TO SERVE WITH LOVE

TO SERVE WITH

By Jo Montgomery

Experience in Soul-to-Soul Service

361
M.1875

Library of Congress Catalog Card No. 73-92488
ISBN 0-8309-0117-5

Printed in the United States of America

Table of Contents

Introduction

by Dr. Roy H. Schaefer*

Jesus, on one occasion, is recorded to have washed the feet of his disciples. This act, symbolized in the use of a basin, water, and a towel, was shared on the evening of the Passover preparation and the communion. The written scripture suggests that Jesus said, "If I do not wash you, you have no part in me. . . . For I have given you an example, that you also should do as I have done to you" (John 13:8, 15, RSV). In this simple yet dynamic act Jesus actualized his view of souls (persons). He also vividly exemplified that the best use of our souls is to willingly and meaningfully share ourselves as friends and servants with others.

The recent past few years have given me the opportunity to contact people in various parts of the world. These have included assignments to the Republic of Haiti, South and East India, the Republic of Honduras, Republic of Nigeria, Republic of Korea, with shorter visits in Guatemala, Israel, Great Britain, Japan, and Alaska. During this time I have also had the privilege of working with thirteen Health Teams which volunteered to serve in the Republic of Haiti and four in the Republic of Honduras. In addition, I've contacted and conversed with competent, dedicated people who are sharing their talents, skills, resources, and "lives" with others in

*Coordinator for Missions Health Foundation, Inc.

various significant avenues of ministry. Many have orally and in written form affirmed the change of attitudes, perspective, and understanding of persons of other cultures that has ensued. Yes, the process of transformation has accelerated and lives have been enriched, as has my own.

In this context it has become more apparent than ever before that a soul gains immeasurably in worth (value) when communication and caring relationships develop. The reciprocal serve-and-be-served, give-and-receive, two-way process is the most important. It is my growing conviction that there is in reality very little I can do for or to someone that will help another to enjoy the more "abundant life." Rather I find this possible in the interaction of two or more persons as they blend their gifts, talents, abilities, and resources *with* one another.

In my better moments, as I reflect on my own life—its joys, hopes, and assured victory with Christ—I am confronted with the awareness that the growing edge of my soul, my outlook, my actions have been most challenging when I have diligently sought to develop such relationships. Dr. James Turpin sensed this when he wrote, "Happiness is as close as you can find someone to love," and speaking of people he wanted very much to serve in another culture came to the insightful assurance, "I needed them as much as they needed me."

When we view another human soul, what do we see— *first?* Do we see shape, form, hairstyle, clothes, color, mannerisms, stature, class, deformity, political bent, religious affiliation? Or do we first see God there? He is there, for his life is vouchsafed to every human soul, and "one being is as precious in his sight as the other" (Jacob 2:27). In all of us he sees sonship and daughtership. Dare we see less than this? He calls everyone ("all are called"), and each has a "right" to participate.

8

How, then, does this reciprocal process work? Perhaps some paraphrased interpolation of life experiences in our world will provide clues.

A village child, following an immunization, took the hand of a health team member and said, "I'm sure proud to know you, Ma'am."

A very elderly lady rushed out of her thatched-roofed home to share a basket of fruit with a dentist—and he graciously accepted her gift.

For his people an African church leader writes: "Silver and gold we have not, but we ask you to accept these small gifts as tokens of our appreciation for your coming to see us as friends, brothers, and co-workers together in God's vineyard." And feeling entirely unworthy, we took their gifts of love—a festival garment, yams, and a live goat.

I've glimpsed the meaning of the worth of souls in the dedicated life of a sexagenarian L.P.N. from Missouri who has served six years in rural areas of Central America, and in a younger R.N. midwife from Australia who is serving her tenth year in the Orient.

I've sensed God's concern for persons in the sharing of public ministry in other cultures when the interpreted verbiage was enriched by the gift of "interpretation of tongues."

A student nurse, friend of the church, serving on a health mission, affirms, "Graceland College and the Division of Nursing experiences have found culmination in the service of this Health Team. These are the quality of people I want to align my life with." And she has!

Villagers in a mountainous area of an island in the Caribbean, in order to show their appreciation of the health teams coming, on their own initiation hewed out roadways with machetes so the jeep could carry personnel and supplies closer to where "bush clinics" would be set up.

Before participating, a physician accepted on a Health Team wrote: "I trust my faith is sufficient that when necessity arises I will be able to do what is required of me, and that my Lord and my associates will have no excuse for embarrassment because I am found wanting."

A mountain village leader said, "We know we are poor, but we don't want you just to do something for us; let us discuss what we can agree to do together."

What is a soul worth? A quantitative determination could be made for each element of the physical body, but this would vary in different areas—and it would ignore worth in qualitative considerations and so would be wholly meaningless.

The relationships of value each of us need to form are the fields of opportunity resident in the "soil" of souls. Our task—should we choose to commit ourselves to it—is to be planters of the seed. We are called to nurture it, to nourish it, to provide it loving care, and to let God "grow it after his likeness." The growing soul will in turn nourish others.

What is a soul worth? Of one thing we can be very sure. It is of infinite worth in the sight of God. It can be the same for us.

I am just beginning to grasp the great investment God has shared in each soul to discover the infinite joy in serving—with love.

CHAPTER ONE

The Name of the Game

The Judeo-Christian religion, by its very nature, is based on love. "God is love." If we believe this, then there is no other name for the game we Christians play.

Christian love is based on service—service that reaches out to all around us. If we are truly Christian we are so filled with love and joy that we cannot contain it—we have to give it away. If we try to bottle it up inside ourselves, one of two things may happen: the pressure may become so great that it will explode in all directions without wise channeling, or it may wither and die from lack of nurture. This is the great paradox: the more we give away of love the more we have left.

William Barclay in his book *Daily Celebration* put it simply and beautifully:

The Christian life cannot be the selfish and self-centered life; it must be the life of care and concern. The great quality of the Christian life is mercy. To be really Christian, we must care so much for others that we forget ourselves and get right into them until we can see with their eyes and feel with their hearts and think with their minds. We must turn so that we are looking outward and not inward.

People need people. This is a book to show how we can meet each other's needs, share each other's problems, carry each other's burdens. It is not a "how-to" book that details

11

specific ways to perform particular services. Rather, it simply tells the ordinary and sometimes extraordinary things that people are doing to help other people.

Some of the projects described here are no longer in existence. Their present existence or lack of it is not the point. The point is that every project was a legitimate answer to a need that existed in that place at that time. The same need may exist in many towns and we may find that the project, modified to meet our circumstances, will answer the need for our community.

Once upon a time, according to the poet James Russell Lowell, there was a young knight preparing to set out in search of the Holy Grail. On the night before he was to leave on his quest, he had a vision of what would happen. He saw himself leaving his castle—young, brave, confident. As he crossed the drawbridge, he was stopped by a disfigured leper who begged for alms. Sir Launfal, revolted by the appearance of the leper, arrogantly threw a gold coin onto the ground beside him.

Then, still in the vision, he saw himself returning home many years later. Now he was old and frail and had suffered failure. When he got back to his castle he found that even his lands and title had been taken over by someone else. Camped on the bank of a frozen stream, he was again accosted by a begging leper. This time, as a result of his own suffering and failure, he was no longer arrogant. All he had to give was a moldy crust of bread, but he broke it in half to share and dipped up a wooden bowlful of water from the icy stream to wash it down.

When he gave the bread and water to the leper, the disfigured beggar changed into the Christ, whose message to

Sir Launfal is the central theme of this book. We should keep it foremost in our minds as we read each chapter.

> Not what we give, but what we share . . .
> For the gift without the giver is bare;
> Who gives of himself with his alms feeds three . . .
> Himself, his hungering neighbor, and Me.

We must give of ourselves . . . always. In the final analysis, that is all we have to give.

CHAPTER TWO

Organized Group Help

[1] *"You're not God, are you?"

This was the most thrilling and humbling question ever addressed to me. The young lady on the other end of the telephone was more serious than facetious. It was one of those unique occasions when an unusual rapport had been established during an all-night shift on Life-line. Not completely rational yet nearly so at a particular point near the end of an hour-long conversation, her voice became hushed as the spiritual uplift we were both experiencing reached its high point. Her voice faltered, and she took a deep breath as the full significance of it all seemed to dawn upon her.

"You're not God, are you?"

Of course she knew it was not God she was speaking to but discerning his Presence in a very real way for a moment she equated him with the person on the other end of the line. I have never walked away from a shift on the Sydney "Help Is as Near as the Telephone" service more elated than I did that morning.

On another occasion I was clutching at straws. Experience suggested strongly that the young man speaking from

---

*Superior numbers at the beginning of sections are keyed to a list of authors who have shared their experiences and thus made this book possible. The list appears on pages 252, 253.

the other side of Harbor Bridge was a genuine potential suicide and might well be, as he said, "shark bait" before the night was out. I was able to get him to give the location of the public telephone he was calling from before I wrote down, stalling as much as possible, the brief note he wanted sent to his wife and children. It was only years of experience that enabled me to calm him into waiting a few minutes longer while I organized a trouble team to go to him. Strangely enough, these tactics often do work. I tell a caller that it will take the team half an hour to get there so he still has plenty of time to disappear into the night if he wants to do so. Feeling free to leave enables him to stay a little longer, irrespective of what happens later.

But now I had done all this and the big question was how to hold him in conversation for the full half hour or more. It so happened that the previous day I had arrived home from a church conference in Mount Macedon in Victoria where there had been a billiard table at the guest house. Between sessions someone suggested a game of snooker but no one knew the rules exactly. This flashed through my mind as I lifted the phone again.

"You still there, Ray?" He was, and I sighed with relief. Desperately I asked, "What sort of snooker player are you?"

"What makes you ask?" he countered.

I told him. Thanks be to God, Ray was an expert snooker player, having reached the last eight in the previous year's championship of another state. The despondent monologue of a moment ago now developed into an animated discussion, and I have never been so happy to learn the rules of a game inside out as I was then. By the time the trouble team arrived, Ray was cooperative and ready to accept the help he so desperately needed.

These are only two of hundreds of similar experiences I

have had since joining the Life-line movement some five or six years ago. Not all telephone calls have ended in success; some have been failures. There have been hoax calls; the dreary, unnecessary ones; trivial calls when I would rather snatch a bit of sleep; and the hopeless psychiatric and drug cases where the only motive for the call was to sound off against society. But some have been worth all the time and inconvenience and sleepless nights a thousand times over.

How did it all start? Members of my congregation in Sydney, Australia, decided to emphasize direct giving and community service as substitutes for fund-raising activities. A few of us tried the Royal Blind Society, but we discovered that its chief emphasis was on fund raising and it already had experts who could beat us hands down at that game. Too, the spirit of independence among the blind themselves was strong, and we thought it was best to let them do as much as they could for themselves. So we put our names down for caring ministry. A few small jobs came our way. I helped with transport and my wife visited a shut-in for some years until the woman died, but there was not much to do. It came to the point where an annual donation seemed to satisfy requirements.

Something more seemed to be required of us than seemed available through the Blind Society if we were to fulfill the urges within us. I had heard about Life-line, so I phoned up and got all the particulars about joining. Other responsibilities delayed me for some time, but eventually I joined the Life-line training course. We had to attend lectures by welfare workers, psychologists, experienced telephone counselors, and ministers of the sponsoring church, as well as being involved in role playing and sit-in sessions for a period of three months, followed by psychology tests and personal interviews before being accepted. Involved with us were members of various denominations.

After gaining telephone experience, I discovered that the best way for me to fit in was to do the night shift once every four weeks. It was tiring, but I found that by staying in town after work at the office all day and snatching a few hours sleep before going on the 10:00 p.m. to 8:00 a.m. shift I could usually survive the next day at the office. Over the years I have become so used to this ritual that I often feel no aftereffects at all.

These years have also seen an enrichment of my life, and ministry in my church has been broadened and enhanced by the sum total of encounter with life in a variety of ways. I am deeply grateful for the opportunities for service that Life-line and the church afford. Life-line is not a complete answer to people's needs, but it meets a very real need in this age. The ultimates of God's kingdom beckon us on, but if the immediates are ignored there can be no future at all.

Indeed, it is our attention to the urgent immediates that will enable us to build the ultimate of God's Kingdom. Many people, like Mr. Selden, find their niche in service through an already existing organization. Nearly every large city has a special telephone listing similar to Life-line. Those who are interested in this field of service should call a local mental health clinic, medical association, or drug abuse agency for the name of the service in their area. The number may be listed in the telephone directory in many ways such as Crisis Clinic, Teen-age Hot Line, Suicide Prevention, Drug Abuse, or Listening Ear.

[2] "Listening Ear . . . may I help you?" I said into the phone. There was no answer. "Hello, this is Listening Ear. May I help you?" Still there was no answer. My mind raced . . . was this a suicide? I was working this Thanksgiving vacation shift alone. "Hello," I said again. "This is Don at the Listening Ear. I'm glad you called. I'd really like to talk to

you. I'm working alone, and no one has called yet this morning."

Then a faint voice spoke brokenly, "Hello, is this really Listening Ear?"

I judged it to be the voice of a teen-age girl. I thought it probably was a suicide case so I flipped the file case in front of me to "Suicide" as I said, "Yes, this is certainly Listening Ear. How are you this morning?"

The story evolved from there. She was a college student nearly a thousand miles from home. Her roommates had left for Thanksgiving vacation, and she was alone in her apartment for the long weekend. She had walked late into the night to pass the time until she started to feel strange. Then she returned to her room and lay on her bed, but she continued to feel worse. None of her friends were in town, but she had heard that Listening Ear was always there to help. She attempted to place a call, but instead found herself talking to her own head sitting on the nightstand with the telephone in position for it to talk to her. They argued with each other at length, with her head berating her for allowing herself to be left alone for four days and telling her how worthless she really was. She decided to ignore it, so she turned the radio on. Her own voice came from the radio as well. She tried to turn it off, but the volume increased, the language became vile, and the berating continued. She turned on the lamp. It became brighter and brighter until it was almost blinding. Then it seemed to dart in and out at her. The radio continued to get louder and also seemed to be attacking her. Her head stayed on the nightstand, grinning and cheering the attacking radio and lamp. She didn't know how long that continued, but eventually it stopped. She lay back exhausted. Again she tried to call Listening Ear. This time she reached me but, understandably, was unsure if she had really reached Listening Ear or if this was merely another

18

hallucination. We talked at length. It had been more than three months since she had used LSD and she had had flashbacks before . . . but never as long or as intense as this. As we talked, her voice grew stronger and so did her confidence. She got up and put the teakettle on to heat. She said she was sure she would be okay now. She gave me her phone number so I could contact her if she didn't call back around noon. Then we hung up. I closed the suicide file and breathed a sigh of relief.

I poured a cup of coffee and stared out into the rainy Thanksgiving morning and prayed. I prayed a prayer of petition for the girl who had called and a prayer of thanksgiving for the forty hours of training Listening Ear volunteers receive to prepare them to deal with drug emergencies and other problems. And I was thankful for the people who had volunteered to man the phones . . . college students, adult members of the community of all educational levels, and even a senior citizen who had learned to listen to kids in trouble.

My prayer was interrupted by the phone. This time it was a man . . . probably in his fifties . . . who was emotionally distraught. His youngest son was home in bed, strung out on drugs of some kind. It had happened before, but when the father had tried to talk to the son about the drug problem, the son called his father an alcoholic. As we talked about the drinking problem, the man tearfully admitted that he was an alcoholic. We talked of where help was available for him. Then we talked about the son's drug problem and how he might best be helped and we discussed the need for honest, open communication between the two. I hung up knowing that the problem had not been solved but at least a possible solution had been presented and there was hope.

The phone rang only twice more during that four-hour shift. A teen-ager wanted a job during Christmas vacation and needed help getting one. I quickly flipped to the Temporary Employment section of the file and provided her with four possibilities. The girl with the flashback made the other call to say that she was fine . . . and also to say "thanks."

There would be other four-hour shifts at other times of the day. Teen-agers who weren't getting along with their parents would call. Teen-agers who had terminated a romance would call. There would be calls about venereal disease and unwanted pregnancy and the need for legal advice and on and on. But most of all, there would be calls from people who were lonely and confused and who needed a listening ear.

My replacement came. I drove home through the rain and prayed again. "Thank you, God, for Listening Ear and thank you for letting me be a part of it." This Thanksgiving Day I was truly thankful.

For those who intend to get into the arena of service via activity in large group projects, there are three facets to be considered:

First, somebody has to originate the organization. Somebody has to see the need and move to organize a group to meet it. For example, it took one housewife in Terre Haute, Indiana, to see that spasmodic paper and glass collections were not doing a worthwhile job for ecology. She proceeded to found Terre Haute Reclamation of Waste. With energy and executive ability, she located a collection center, organized a corps of workers to man the station at designated hours, arranged publicity in the local newspapers and, through the radio and TV stations, found markets for the papers, bottles, and aluminum cans. Proceeds were used to pay rent on the center and trucks (when they were not donated). Only her immediate circle of friends know Mrs. Ed Warner, but thousands in the Terre Haute area have heard about "Mrs. Throw."

* * *

Hidden Springs in Ontario was the product of a minister's dream. For years the Reverend Ralph Howlett dreamed of a place where troubled people could come and live in a Christian atmosphere with physical and psychiatric care available as they needed it. With financial support from Christian friends, he acquired a suitable house and found Christian psychiatrists and counselors who were willing to donate time and service to help him.

Guests—never called or treated as patients—lived in a family atmosphere of love and concern. Others came in once a day for therapy. This Recovery Group could be compared to Alcoholics Anonymous except that it was for people with mental and emotional problems. Each day time was provided for a Christian devotional period, occupational therapy, psychodrama sessions, and personal counseling with the psychiatrist or a trained counselor. As each guest improved, he was encouraged to perform assigned work duties to rebuild his sense of purpose and worth in the community.

From the start this was a venture in faith. There was a set fee for guests, but only those who could afford to pay were ever expected to share the expense. No one was ever turned away for lack of money. Contributions from Christian friends made up the deficit each month of operation.

Did it work? Meet Ruby as she presides graciously behind the counter of her boutique in a busy Toronto shopping mall. There is nothing in the appearance of this tall, beautifully groomed woman to suggest the alcoholic, emotionally disturbed failure who went to Hidden Springs some years ago. Mary, a sober drunk, drove Ruby to Hidden Springs in her car, and Ruby vomited all the way. When they arrived, the car . . . and Ruby . . . were a mess. Aghast at the bleary-eyed, sagging wreck standing on the doorstep, smelling of vomit and liquor, one of the volunteer workers gasped, "You don't

21

think we can do anything for her, do you?" Mary kept a tight grip on Ruby's arm to keep her from falling. "That's why I brought her up here."

Today Ruby is completely rehabilitated, sober, married, and able to work and live a well-adjusted life. Part of her newfound happiness is to be active in helping others find what she has found . . . trying to do for them what has been done for her. If anyone asks, she will tell him, "I wouldn't be here if it wasn't for the grace of God . . . and Hidden Springs."

And Hidden Springs was founded by one man with the vision and drive to make his dream become reality.

* * *

Second, every service organization needs volunteer help. No organization is any stronger or any more effective than its core of willing workers. Anyone looking for an organization through which to serve his community should consider those which are well established and which have proved their worth: Goodwill, Salvation Army, Red Cross, United Fund, March of Dimes, Gideons, service clubs (Kiwanis, Rotary, Lions, etc.), fraternal lodges (Masonic, Moose, Elk, etc.).

Some may become workers for special organizations because of personal contact and interest. For example, many people may have a friend or relative afflicted by a specific disease, and this leads them to become volunteer workers for the foundation which helps these victims or which funds research. Typical among these are the Multiple Sclerosis Foundation, Muscular Dystrophy Foundation, and Heart Fund. An example of how an individual may become involved in one of these organizations is in the experience of Madolynn Burlington.

While I was a member of the General Council of Women for my church, I became acquainted with a church family whose little girl suffered from cystic fibrosis, a disease which is inherited and—at this time—incurable. It seemed to me that I just had to do something to help. I could not be content to stand by and watch. My first job was as county chairman in the yearly drive for funds for research. I knew many of the local church leaders, and as they were asked they responded as chairmen in their vicinities. They in turn obtained church women in their own areas to be block chairmen and door-to-door campaigners. While serving on the Council of Women, I had assignments to out-of-town retreats and family camps as far away as Canada; these afforded me an opportunity to publicize and urge persons to join in the fight against this terrible disease. The response was heartwarming. In Florida, Oregon, Texas, Michigan, and other states, generous people have responded. The people of Hawaii are a great strength and provide an enormous contribution toward research funds.

Church camp facilities seemed ideal to permit these youngsters with their doctors' permission to have a few days reprieve from normal home routine. Great care was taken to assure complete protection during this Christian oriented "vacation" for our young guests. Church youth gave wonderful cooperation as they worked with the children on a one-to-one basis. Nurses, cooks, counselors, directors, and teachers, all became a dedicated team to make it a carefully programmed four days of fun for the children; for many patients this was the first time to be away from home overnight. Publicity about the camp helped to educate more people about cystic fibrosis and suggest how they could assist in the fight against it.

Many times God himself seems to lead us to a particular area of service. Such was the case with Mary Edythe Baker

when she became involved in working with schools for retarded children.

There are experiences in life that seem divinely directed. It's like going down a long corridor and finding all the rooms are locked except the one that God intends you to enter. Here you receive a challenge and an opportunity to be partners with him in a new adventure. That's how it was with me.

At last I was going to have a year in which I could please myself. I'd been offered a job as a nursery-school assistant five mornings a week, and I planned to enroll in a decorative sewing class at night school. This plus my home and three children were all that I could manage, so I decided to terminate all church and social activities at the end of June, leaving me free in September. This year I was not going to do for God—I was going to do for myself.

Well, the Lord has a great sense of humor, and mid-September was the jester. The first blow came by letter. It read, "Due to a smaller enrollment than expected we cannot afford to hire another teacher at this time. We hope to be in better circumstances by November and will . . ."

Oh, well, I thought, with all this free time I'll just volunteer for Children's Aid. However, I was told that I wasn't needed at that time, but that I would be put on the standby list. . . .

"Oh, well," I said to my husband Ken, "I still have night school." Registration night came and, after a long wait in line, I discovered that I was enrolled number 21 in a class limited to 20.

"However," I was told, "you'll be the first on our substitute list. . . ." I cried all the way home. I just couldn't believe it.

That Wednesday, as I was glancing through our local

newspaper, an advertisement caught my eye. "Volunteers Needed for Nursery School for Retarded Children—one morning a week, 9:00 to 11:30 a.m."

It was the right job, the right time, the right place. I applied and was assigned to serve Fridays, starting that very week.

My first experience with retardation was one of survival. The teacher had decided that the four severely retarded youngsters were disruptive to the program and slowed down the learning progress of the trainable children. Their classwork was devoted to language, small motor skills, toilet training, and independent action in caring for themselves. The four children requiring special care did not fit in. A room was provided for them with only one volunteer to look after all their needs—usually the newest or the strongest. If you could survive a morning in there, you could survive anything. It was chaos for mind and muscle. I used to go home . . . and to bed. In fact, the only thought that kept me going was that if their parents could stand it twenty-four hours a day, I could surely stand it one morning a week. I was also perturbed because there was no time to give each child the individual attention he so desperately needed. It soon became apparent that I was just baby-sitting—a repugnant idea no matter how much parents appreciated the relief. There had to be a better way.

At this time there were four nurseries operating in Toronto under the auspices of the Metro Toronto Association for the Retarded. Nurseries were a new field for them, too, so we were all feeling our way along together. As a start, we were asked to set up our own executive council, and in October I was persuaded to take the job of treasurer. In November we learned that, although the parents paid according to their means, the cost of running the schools was prohibitive for the association and we were encouraged to become as self-supporting as possible. Our expenses were high. We used cabs because car pools had proved unsatisfactory, and our teachers were specialists and paid accordingly. The deficit for each school was $4000. "Well, Lord," I prayed, "where do we go from here?" I forgot that man's extremity is God's opportunity.

In February there was a request for people to man a booth at the flower show at O'Keefe's Center for the Arts. We would be selling roses, and the proceeds would go to the association. I agreed to do a shift and was surprised to learn, upon my arrival, that it was rose bushes, not roses, that I was selling. The light went on, and I knew how we were going to raise money for our schools.

The plan thrilled everyone at the executive meeting. It would be a twofold campaign of fund-raising and education. It is ever a battle to make the public aware of the difference between mental retardation and mental illness. Flowers would be sold on all the plazas in the east end in a gigantic one-day blitz. The other nurseries decided to join us, and it became a city-wide venture. The flower growers could not give us roses in May, and the heat of June would wilt them too quickly.

"Too bad you don't want carnations," the manager said. "We have them coming out our ears in June."

"I'll take them!" I said, surprised at my own voice, and Carnation Day was born.

It is now in its ninth year. I served as chairman four times and tried hard to mold a workable team of various faiths. God blessed us and we were able to see that a difference of name or idea still referred to the same Power, and we were able to pray together in sincerity and faith. It was an experience, but our goal of becoming self-supporting was never reached because each year we kept opening new schools. Our waiting lists are long and constant.

I was school chairman the second year. The severely retarded children still needed special care. Our school was not equipped to handle them and the few we did have were there for extenuating parent relief. The volunteer enrollment was increased, and the teacher devised a "big muscle program" to be used so that something constructive began to happen. We had to have a team of five volunteers per child—one for each day. We also had to make opportunities for these people to get together for discussions of their mutual children. Log books kept on each child were full of observations and successes. We began a volunteer training program which explained why we used routine procedures and how. A library was made available, and we were encouraged to familiarize ourselves with the different types of retardation. We also visited schools and institutions to see what life could be for our children.

The following year the association was ready to take another step. Two special care nurseries were set up for the severely retarded. It was my privilege to recruit volunteers and guide the operational procedures of both until they got going. One was intercity, and the other was established in my own church in Scarborough.

Another area that has demanded my attention over the past few years is the unwed, retarded mother. But my main involvement is participating on a board made up of doctors, lawyers, social workers, teachers, and "laymen." We listen to problems and try to reach constructive recommendations. We hope to initiate changes in procedures and laws that will enhance the opportunities of the retarded to achieve their God-given right of reaching their individual potential.

It is hard work being a volunteer in this field, but it is also rewarding. Success is often slow in coming—sometimes months, sometimes years—but when it comes we weep with the joy of it. Sympathy is not needed—just confident expectancy. We give no more help than is absolutely required, and we learn to speak without chatter. Our hearts go out not to the severely retarded child who is relatively happy within his limited world but to the mildly retarded one who faces the constant bewilderment of never being able to fit in and not understanding why. For this reason we try to teach the trainable children to pray and to have an awareness of God in hope that they will never feel completely alone.

The years of service have taught me to appreciate many things that I once took for granted. Sharing my experiences at home has helped us to keep many of our personal problems in their proper perspective. We have been greatly blessed. I have learned what it means to do something truly meaningful, and it is a ruler by which I measure my spare time activities even today.

There is nothing like the experience of hearing a small child discover he has a voice. When I am holding a special care child in my arms or working his large muscles for him, I look into his eyes and become aware of the worth of his soul.

Once a mother said to me, "Mrs. Baker, why do you do this? You don't have a retarded child, do you?"

"That's why I do it, Mrs. X," I replied, putting my arm around her shoulder, "because I don't have one."

It has truly been an adventure with God. I shall never be the same again because of it.

Most hospitals are grateful for the volunteer help of Candy Stripers, Gray Ladies, and Auxiliaries. Working in this capacity can be exciting and rewarding service.

* * *

[3] As a Red Cross Gray Lady or volunteer for twenty-one years, I have given thousands of hours of service in the

Independence Sanitarium and Hospital and in Blood Bank activities at the Red Cross Headquarters in Kansas City as well as with the Mobile Units.

Gray Ladies in the hospital do much visiting with the patients as well as performing services which relieve the nurses for more important patient care. Personally I have always felt that the visiting was the most important feature of our work.

One day while I was making my assigned rounds, I went into a private room to find no flowers. The patient, nurses had told me, had suffered a complete nervous breakdown and the doctors held no hope for his recovery. In fact, the doctors felt that when he recovered enough to leave the hospital he would have to be confined in a mental institution.

As I entered the room, he seemed completely withdrawn. He did not even hear my words of greeting. I stood beside his bed and continued to talk quietly to him. When I asked how he was feeling, he finally responded with a slight shake of the head. I asked if there was anything I could get or do for him. Again there was another negative shake of the head. Finally I asked him what he was interested in. "What would you be doing right now if you were well and out of the hospital?" He continued to shake his head. Then reluctantly he admitted that he used to like to go hunting.

I remembered some books I had which were published by the National Geographic Society concerning hunting with a camera instead of a gun. I told him about them and asked if he would like to read them. He replied, "I might," but showed no real interest.

As I live near the hospital I went home and got the books, praying that a miracle might take place and that this man might be healed so he could return to his family. I visited with him a few minutes more and then left his room.

Several days later as I was busy cleaning the front of my

house I happened to glance up from my work and saw a man coming up the steps. I did not recognize him, but I did recognize the books he was carrying under his arm.

He greeted me cordially, introduced himself, and recalled our visits in the hospital. He thanked me repeatedly for those visits and my kindness in loaning him the books which he had thoroughly enjoyed reading. His big news was that the doctors had released him and that he was returning to his home.

Truly God still does work miracles.

* * *

And sometimes we can play a small part in God's miracles by being alert to opportunities to serve.

It isn't necessary to be an alcoholic to assist in the program—although it helps. A later chapter will tell the story of "drunks helping drunks," but here is the story of what happened to and through a minister who frequently counsels alcoholics and their families:

* * *

[4] Shortly after I entered into active counseling of the alcoholic and his family, I was asked to attend the Christmas Eve candlelight service of Alcoholics Anonymous, where members tell of their gratitude for sobriety during the past year. My responsibility was to tie together these expressions into the message of God's love for his creation in the birth, life, and death of Christ. Forty-five persons participated in that testimonial service with forty-four voicing their thanks for the blessing of sobriety. One of the group (an avowed atheist) left during the service.

Two months later a psychiatrist called to tell me that this man had been admitted to a hospital the previous Christmas Eve and confined to inpatient care. Now, his doctor said, he had just uncovered his patient's deep desire to kill me, and he felt that I should be aware of this. It was not my usual nature to do so, but I calmly asked the doctor how I could help. The next morning the three of us met at the hospital, and for over an hour discussed the problem, which centered around the patient's belief that I had influenced the forty-four people to make their statements about God's love and direction in their lives, rather than such being their own feelings. He said, "Charles, I like you as an individual, but I hate what you represent so much that I would kill you if I ever took a drink." Despite this threat, I experienced a peaceful feeling beyond my ability to explain or describe.

Two weeks later he was released from the hospital and returned to his job, and in the following years A.A. members would tell me that in closed meetings (which only alcoholics can attend and where personal problems are discussed) they had noted a change coming over this man; he even indicated a deep desire to understand God.

Some five years after the initial experience I was invited by several members to attend the Christmas Eve candlelight service at another location; this time I was not to be a speaker but a guest. I accepted, and on arriving that night I found nearly a hundred people gathered; among them was this ex-atheist. When the service started I was surprised to note that he was serving as chairman, and, as was the custom, he called on each person in turn to speak. When it came my turn he passed by, asking the next person to speak. I felt no resentment when this happened, but I wondered if a barrier still existed between us. However, when the last person had spoken, he turned to me and said: "Charles, I passed you by because I wanted you to tie together the messages of this service, the birthday celebration of two persons attaining their first and second years of sobriety, and the message of Christmas."

Whatever I said that beautiful night were not my words, because I was caught completely unaware of my responsibility, but I know it was adequate because God knew my needs, and directed me through this meaningful experience with joy and thankfulness and love. Afterwards the chairman asked everyone to stand, and as is always the custom in A.A. meetings, we repeated in unison the Lord's Prayer to conclude the service. How wonderful it is to realize that because of God's love and concern for his children I was directed to do the right thing at the right time in this unusual encounter.

A little known but growing organization is spreading Christian love and concern across the world. Here is an account of what it means to "FISH."

[5] "FISH. It's a way to let your light shine!" If someone had said this to me three years ago I would have questioned such senseless advice. "Rainbow trout" might have been the first thought to cross my mind along with my lack of enthusiasm—and skill—for the sport of fishing.

Since January of 1971 when my husband, Dale, and I were intrigued by a newspaper article about a good-neighbor volunteer movement called "FISH," I have found "FISHing" not only possible but exciting. This same newspaper article about the only FISH chapter in this area triggered the beginning of eight other FISH chapters in Metropolitan Denver including two in the west area in the city itself and one in the east half.

In less than a year during the formation of the East Denver FISH Chapter, my husband and I saw interest grow from four individuals in three different denominations to 175 individuals from thirty different churches. During this time we worked with a steering committee of less than a dozen people, as a unit, with the common bond of the love of Christ, obtaining a twenty-four-hour answering service telephone number and taking close to one hundred requests for help the first month.

The FISH idea originated in England in 1961 when both pastor and people were convinced that old-fashioned neighborliness was waning and that something must be done about it. Soon news of this unique way of expressing Christian concern for others spread to other European countries and even to South Africa and Japan. In 1964 it crossed the Atlantic to Springfield, Massachusetts. Now there are 1,000 known FISH chapters throughout the world including Canada, Mexico, England, Wales, Northern Ireland, and Sweden besides the United States. An accurate count is not possible because there is no national structure to the FISH movement.

The purpose of FISH is twofold. FISH makes it possible for people who want to *give* help and people who *need* help to get together. It is a channel through which love and concern for others can be shown . . . not just voiced. FISH gives our prayers feet! It's a way to say "I care" that makes a difference.

FISH made a difference when . . .

A young couple from Wyoming found themselves without food and shelter in Portland, Oregon. Someone told them to call FISH. They had never heard of it before. Now they can't say enough good about it.

A woman in her hospital room called for help from FISH for her roommate whose illness was prolonged, whose house had burned down, and whose husband had been in a car accident while she was in the hospital.

In one month's time East Denver FISH answered seventy-five requests for transportation to hospitals, clinics, and supermarkets for the elderly and ill; another thirty requests for food; and between seventy and eighty miscellaneous calls including a number of referrals.

Stranded travelers in Effingham, Illinois, were helped on their way with the following note and a little traveling money: "Dear Friend, it has been our privilege to try to help you. . . . We believe that the Lord is the true Source of help to those in need. We are only instruments at this time and place. He has many, many others. We pray that if you should need help again, He will put you in touch with someone to provide it. You have our personal prayer for a safe journey and for God's blessings in the future. Sincerely, FISH."

An elderly woman received emergency treatment at midnight in a hospital for an accidental injury. She and her husband had no way to get home, no money, no relatives or friends in Denver. A nurse knew about FISH.

A family on a diet of beans for three days was given several sacks of groceries.

A couple with five children, the youngest less than a month old, were going from Iowa to California where a job was waiting for the husband when their car broke down for the third time and they were stranded in Denver. FISH came to their rescue.

A family in Millsboro, Delaware, lost everything in a fire which destroyed their home. FISH was able to find them food, clothing, furniture, and other household items.

A mother and her children came to Denver expecting to meet a relative whom she was unable to find. She camped at the edge of the city with her children for a few days. When she inquired at a filling station about selling her watch for necessary money, she was told to call FISH.

A blind man in utter despair since his wife suddenly died felt helpless and abandoned in his loneliness. A neighbor said, "Call FISH."

An elderly couple, on a pension, from out of town

needed four units of blood. A nurse called FISH for them.

The symbol of the fish is used by all chapters not only because the early Christians used it as a means of identification but also because the Greek word for fish is an acrostic which means "Jesus Christ, God's Son, Savior." The slogan is "Love thy neighbor," and volunteers recognize that their neighbor is anyone who needs them.

My major responsibility in the East Denver chapter has been to give slide presentations to various churches and other groups to obtain volunteers and financial support for answering service expenses. This has given me many rich spiritual experiences as I have heard members of other denominations speak of the function of the Holy Spirit in their lives and of their anticipation of the coming of Christ. To have new friends who have such a deep relationship with the Master—some giving themselves in complete dedication to serving their fellowmen—brings joy which is hard to express in words. To see husbands and wives and whole families working together as a unit—giving time, energy, and finances because "FISH is the most tangible way of sharing the love of Christ" that they know—is an inspiring experience.

"FISHing" here in Denver has brought enrichment to the lives of each member of our family and to many in our church home. It is truly a way to let our light shine.

* * *

Less church oriented and with an entirely different kind of help to offer are the Family Center for Maternity Care and La Leche Leagues across the country. The first involves classes taught in hospitals by the Red Cross or private groups to give childbirth education to young families. La Leche League tries to inform and help women who want to breast-feed their babies. It offers a series of five free classes on breast feeding and a book entitled *The Womanly Art of*

Breast Feeding for sale through local chapters and the national headquarters.

Women in Lexington, Kentucky, are taking their maternal concern one step further. Under the name "Birthright" they are organizing a twenty-four-hour telephone answering service for mothers with problems. Their aim is to establish a "big sister" relationship. Many young mothers, uneasy and uncertain in their new role, hesitate to call a busy pediatrician with their seemingly unimportant questions and fears. "We want them to feel free to call us around the clock, no matter how silly their questions may seem to them. If it really is unimportant, we can reassure them. If it sounds at all disturbing, we can get them medical help fast."

Individual church congregations around the world are becoming increasingly active in all forms of social service. It would be impossible to compile a definitive list of the work being done. The services mentioned here are not the only ones being performed; they are simply intended to be representative of the services needed in many communities. Perhaps other congregations could undertake similar projects.

[6] The work of the nationwide Goodwill Industries can be supplemented in many areas by church organizations, as in the Social Service Center in Independence, Missouri. This Center began on a small scale in 1920 when it was known as the Commodity Shop. Since then it has grown into a business where twenty-two paid employees and seventy-five volunteers work together. The average age is seventy-four, but there are some young people on the roll, too. The building in which the Center was relocated in 1970 was converted from an automobile agency by four ex-convicts, five senior citizens, and six high school students. The Social Service Center serves a twofold need. It provides clothing, linens, and furniture at a very minimal price (often for nothing) to those

on limited incomes, and it provides employment for people who have difficulty finding jobs. Typical of the lives touched by the Center are the widow who completely outfitted her three children for school on a ten-dollar bill . . . and the crippled man who started out straightening up shelves and became supervisor of the bargain basement.

Blue Summit, a low-income area located between Kansas City and Independence, Missouri, is frequently referred to as Dogpatch. Here homes are often in need of repair . . . and so are the people who live in them. A woman who grew up in Dogpatch and went on to better things appealed to her church group to help. "These people need the gospel," she said, "but first they need help in homemaking and hygiene and family relations." As a result of her concern, Project LIFT (low-income family training) was instituted, and a call went out for volunteers to conduct classes in cooking, sewing, budget-planning, child care, small motor repair, reupholstery, grooming, and weight control (the high starch diet of low-income families often results in overweight which in turn breeds poor health and low morale). Once-a-week classes were held in a nearby church, but much of the teaching took place on location. A volunteer carpenter spent his Saturdays teaching Dogpatchers to repair their homes. Women with cars provided transportation to grocery stores for LIFT women and, when asked, offered shopping suggestions. Some regularly visited the area to help housewives become more efficient homemakers . . . sharing tips on cleaning and meal preparations from government surplus commodities. The project coordinator, a psychologist, provided free counseling, and two registered nurses volunteered as hygiene instructors. One of the most appreciated services was a class in hair care and styling by two beauticians. Typical of the lift provided by LIFT was voiced by a mother, "I was a big, fat woman with no pride. Since losing sixty pounds and learning how to 'fix up' I feel like a new person." Now she too is an instructor; she heads up what she calls the Big Sister program for the girls in Blue Summit who want to be more attractive. Thus the love of Christ went to Dogpatch . . . and many families are happier because of it.

Better Selections, Inc., is a private introduction service for Christian single adults. These introductions are a means for potentially compatible men and women to become acquainted. As a part of enrollment, clients complete a questionnaire. This information is analyzed and compared with that of others. They are introduced when there is reasonably close correspondence among the various factors analyzed. The service is available to adults of any Christian faith. In November of 1969 the first introductions were mailed out. Many friendships developed, and in the first two years of its operation over a dozen marriages resulted from these friendships.

A church building known as the Belmont Street Mission was closed when the Negro congregation merged with the white congregation in Pensacola, Florida. The building was offered to the Community Action Program for whatever purpose it would best serve in the area. After necessary repairs and improvements had been made, the building was reopened as the West Side Center. It has been a busy place ever since. Classes in cooking, sewing, and first aid are offered, along with arts and crafts. Among the attractions are murals painted on the walls by neighborhood artists. A full-time VISTA worker is in charge of the center, but many volunteers offer their assistance. One is a blind girl who comes in each Friday to read from a Braille storybook to children who live in the area. Her young listeners are very protective of her, and a two-way fulfillment of needs has resulted from this "story hour" friendship. As a result of the success of rummage sales held there, a thrift shop has been established. Other services are on the agenda and will be instituted in the near future.

[7] Two young couples founded Christ Center in Lexington, Kentucky. Acting on faith that this was where God wanted them to work, they bought an unused, old building and set about renovating it into living quarters for themselves and meeting rooms for the people of the community. Every month their bills are paid by another miracle . . . somehow the money is there because people who know of this work are "moved" to send them a check. Into Christ Center come the hoods, the drug addicts, the drunks, the derelicts of Lexington who have seen these young Christians witnessing on the street corners and somehow sense that there is another way of life. Of particular interest to the two young women are the children of the area . . . ragged, dirty, smelling of filth and garbage . . . who have never heard the term Jesus Christ used in any way except as swear words. Lives are being changed in this inner city because four young Christians not only care but dare to serve the needy.

Church groups have also been instrumental in establishing projects to serve young people, ranging from the camp for children with cystic fibrosis (already mentioned) to camps for the physically handicapped, the mentally handicapped, diabetics, and inner-city children. Some of these have become well established and a few have developed into national enterprises.

[6] A church group in Tahiti, partially funded by the Youth Federation, has set up a youth center on Mount Tiona which features a ball court, day camping facilities, and youth-centered ministries. The camping program has become particularly popular with more than 650 campers and staff

members participating. Several groups have gone to the outer islands to help set up camp programs there.

In July 1970, members of a church in Honolulu, Hawaii, began a recreation program called "Sun and Fun" for children of low-income families in the area. For three hours each Saturday morning games, sports, crafts, drama, and music activities are provided at the church for youngsters five to twelve years old. Supplementing these are field trips and three-day camps at the beach. For children who live in high-rise apartments, this is an important diversion.

Church groups in the Kansas City area have spawned several very active organizations devoted to young people. In 1968 a couple from nearby Atherton offered their farm as the site of a day camp for deprived city children. The "Day in the Country" program now serves well over one thousand children annually and is operated for a two-week period each summer by a volunteer staff of fifty-five youth and fifteen adults. This venture has expanded into the Woodland Hills Youth Foundation which offers weekend and week-long camping trips for junior and senior high students. The Foundation continues to expand its services and now includes a program to provide young people with job training. The Second Coming Shop is a new edition of the old-time store featuring natural foods, bakery goods, mod clothes, posters, and a wide variety of handcrafted items such as leather goods, candles, and artwork. The shop employs eighteen young people who with adult assistance, gain firsthand experience in purchasing, advertising, display, and sales. The advances made in providing job opportunities and vocational training for youth in the greater Kansas City area has encouraged the opening of a similar shop in Iowa. There is no reason why such projects could not be successfully inaugurated in many cities.

The founders of Woodland Hills Youth Foundation have branched out into another project called Adventure Trails which is designed to assist youth between the ages of ten and seventeen who show early symptoms of problem behavior. Through high-adventure camping and small-group techniques the program intercepts children caught in a variety of failure patterns ranging from hostility to withdrawal. Three trained counselors participate fully with ten youth on each trip to help them find more positive images of themselves and more capable ways of relating to others. The twenty-six days are designed to enable the group to help itself. Until recently the project was funded by the government, but since government funds have been cut it has become necessary to charge individuals who want to participate. The staff is still volunteer, but living expenses must, of course, be paid.

An even larger operation, popularly known as Camp Personality, is specifically designed for inner-city children and is government funded for them. Other youngsters may attend also for a fee. This has mushroomed into a national project. However, the local camps are still staffed largely by volunteers: adult church members serve as cooks, camp nurses, and counselors; young people serve as counselors and instructors.

[8] Charles, 11, was small but belligerent. All week long he had been pushing, kicking, and shouting at the other campers. Twice he had been accused of stealing.

Debbie, 12, was thin and sullen. She was a defiant loner who crushed every attempt to involve her in the camp activities. She believed that she had been sent to camp by her mother as a punishment for some unnamed crime.

Tracy, 14, was tough and rebellious. Her counselor had brought her to me because she refused to cooperate with cleaning the cabin. When asked why she was unwilling to help, her only response was "I hate Whites."

Charles, Debbie, and Tracy were not unique at this camp. They and sixty other inner-city youth were attending Camp Personality at Xenia, Illinois. This was the first camping experience for all the campers and each had come with his own unique mixture of sullen, rebellious belligerence.

My position was camper chairman, which meant that I was chief disciplinary officer. In this position, I got to know Charles, Debbie, and Tracy quite well. But they were by no means the only disciplinary problems we had.

Everyone on the staff was driven to the limits of endurance. I had to send counselors in to take a nap because they had exhausted themselves physically and mentally trying to moderate the aggressiveness of the campers.

Wednesday was an especially trying day since we had a cook-out scheduled for that afternoon. As we unloaded the campers at the picnic site, they began an impromptu game of tag. Charles started throwing rocks at the people who tried to tag him. Debbie refused to play, and then began hitting people who ran past her.

I called both Debbie and Charles to me and had them help unload the picnic supplies from my car. Then I told Debbie that she could help start the fire while Charles and I went back for the rest of the supplies.

As I drove I talked to Charles about the things I saw along the road. We stopped the car once to look at some wild day lilies growing in the ditch, and again to sample some wild strawberries. Charles began to talk about sports he enjoyed. By the time we returned to the picnic area, we were friends. Later, as I sat at the campfire, Charles came over to sit beside me.

As the campfire progressed, I saw that Debbie was pinching the girls she was with, so I had her come sit beside me as well. She sat there, pulling clumps of grass out of the ground. I leaned over and whispered, "Debbie, I like you a lot." She turned to me with a puzzled expression and then back to the campfire. But where she had been tense and irritable, she now seemed relaxed.

At the conclusion of the campfire we stood with our hands clasped and sang "Blest be the tie that binds." I stood with Charles on my left and Debbie on my right and felt the extra squeeze that each gave my hand. I looked across the embers of the fire and saw Tracy and her counselor singing together, hand in hand.

When we returned to camp, Charles came to me to return some things that he had "found" during the previous days at camp. Debbie came to tell me that she was going to try harder to get along with her cabin mates. As the campers prepared for bed, I watched Tracy and her counselor walk by with their arms around each other. And I knew that God's Spirit had been present at that campfire.

I have seen many lives changed these past few years at Personality camps. Inner-city youths have come to the camp sullen and defiant but left enthusiastic and responsive. The lives of staff members have been changed as well. Many came to "give something to those unfortunate kids." And then, when they came face-to-face with the campers, they found that they gained as much as they gave: they learned to *really* love. They found that love is not an emotion but a way of acting toward others as if they were individuals worth knowing well. As staff members began to apply this rule, they found to their surprise that the "bad" campers were worth knowing–and loving.

Camp Personality is one avenue of bringing people together so that the force of this love can be expressed in their lives. For me it has proved a very successful means of bringing the redeeming power of God's love into the lives of people.

Women's clubs, both in and out of the church, can render a physical service which is too often neither noticed nor appreciated but which would be sadly missed if it were not there. In many cities and towns these women's clubs cater dinners and luncheons for local service clubs, conventions, and conferences where the need for a reasonable fee makes such catering unattractive for commercial catering services or restaurants. Such an organization is the Laurel Club of Independence, Missouri.

———

[9] The service rendered by the Laurel Club is different than you normally associate with a group of church women, but the physical body has to be ministered to as well as the spiritual. "Marthas" are always needed in the church, staying in the background and doing some of those less glorious things which most people take for granted and do not want to do. Serving meals to the thousands of delegates and visitors who attend the World Conferences of the restored church is no easy or glamorous task.

This service is often hard and tiresome. There have been times when I have been so thoroughly exhausted mentally and physically that I have felt I could not go on any longer. But somehow God has always met my needs, giving me strength so that this service has become a joy instead of a burden. It is a stewardship, a Zionic endeavor in working together in serving others and serving God.

* * *

The third requirement for organizations to work in serving others is that the public knows about them. Individuals must be aware of the organizations and their purposes so they can put needy people in touch with the agencies best equipped to help.

44

[10] One cold November night four years ago my wife Marie and I were driving home from church along a country lane when around a bend the headlights picked out the figure of a tramp thumbing a lift. Instinctively I started to stop, then stepped on the accelerator.

At the next road junction, however, Marie and I looked at each other as she spoke the words in both our minds: "Let's go back and see if we can help." We returned and picked up the man who smelled heavily of alcohol. I asked him where he was going, then began the eight-mile trip to Cotswold Village of Stroud as he had requested.

As we traveled we talked of many things. I learned that he had fought in the Spanish Civil War with the International Socialist Brigade and since that time had drifted around England living rough, sleeping in barns and under hedges, gradually drinking himself to death.

We dropped him off in Stroud, not knowing where he was to sleep (he didn't know himself). As we parted I gave him the only money I had, 13/4d ($1.60), and my visiting card, telling him that he was welcome to call any time he needed help. Marie asked him to spend the little money we had given him on food, but we thought that probably he would buy more spirits to drink. This thought did not deter us for we remembered the admonition: "And ye will not suffer that the beggar putteth up his petition to you in vain and turn him out to perish."

The following evening I was away from home on church business when Marie was visited by this man. She invited him in, and they sat all evening talking. The man confessed the atheism his experiences had led him to. Finally he arose, saying, "I must have a drink now, and as I never drink in front of a lady I will go. But I will return later in the week when your husband is home."

I made many inquiries regarding what could be done to

help this man. I was surprised at the types of ministry and services offered by various churches and social agencies. Anticipating his return, I arranged for him to have a bed at a Church of England hostel for tramps, although a local Catholic monastery offered the same facilities. I arranged for him to go to Bristol to a Methodist center for drying out alcoholics and also obtained admission to a work training center for him when he was finally settled.

The minister in charge of the hostel knew him and warned me that "Murphy" was a wanderer. How right he was, for Murphy never returned to our home, preferring instead to pursue the life of a vagabond to which he was accustomed.

We shall never forget him, however, for his coming into our lives helped us to catch a glimpse of a different world—a world where our values and standards are of no consequence and material things are no attraction.

Murphy also opened our eyes to the universality of God's love working through people of all faiths. The people at the hostel, monastery, alcoholic center, and work training center didn't ask "What denomination is he?" or "What is his social security number?" They were ready and equipped to help him adapt to a way of life that he ultimately chose not to accept.

I'm not sure that we helped Murphy, but his influence on us will always be remembered.

There are three things, then, to be considered by those who become interested in service through organized groups:

1. Somebody has to found the organization. Somebody has to see the need and supply the energy, enthusiasm, and know-how to organize a group to serve that need.

2. A service organization needs workers, usually volun-

teers, who will donate time, talents, and physical resources to perform the actual services.

3. The public must be informed of the services available through the existing organizations. People must be able to make referrals of the needy to agencies equipped to help them.

All of us can help in one or more of these ways. The prime requirements are love, observation, and dedication.

Service organizations in every community need all the help they can get if they are to serve others.

CHAPTER THREE

The Good Neighbor Policy

" We were due to start home from Florida one day last spring, and I chose that particular morning to wake up out-of-sorts, uptight, and with my general nastiness showing. To top it off everything went wrong. I couldn't get the suitcases to shut, nothing tasted right at breakfast, my coffee was cold, I twisted my ankle as we walked out to the car, and I forgot my extra purse in the motel room and had to go back for it.

Of course, all this was my husband's fault ... or so anyone would have thought who could have heard me taking out my temper on him. Poor man ... all he said was an occasional "Now, Mother, keep your hair on."

Then the car wouldn't start—which would be bad enough any time, but this was a Sunday morning and there wasn't a garage open in the whole town. I fussed and fumed. (There is a name for women who act like this; it isn't a nice name, but it's exactly what I was.)

Finally, for no reason at all, the car started and we were on our way, but I griped and growled right on through the day. First air conditioning was too cold, then not cold enough. My husband was driving too fast ... or too slow. He was tailgating the car ahead ... or not keeping up with the stream of traffic. I continued until it could only have been the angels that kept my husband from hitting me.

About four o'clock we started looking for a motel but every one we came to had a "No Vacancy" sign out. That stepped up my flow of unpleasantries. Not only had Byrnes been personally responsible for all my discomforts during the day but now he was going to see to it that we didn't even have a bed to sleep in that night.

We stopped for supper long after dark . . . another bone of contention because Byrnes had *deliberately* passed up all the good restaurants where I had wanted to stop. After a meal of nonstop complaints, I got back into the car . . . and it wouldn't start!

That did it. Sunday night or no Sunday night, there had to be a mechanic somewhere who would fix our car. I left Byrnes sitting behind the wheel and stalked back into the restaurant to find a telephone.

Just as I reached the door a man got out of his car and came toward me. On impulse I stopped him and asked if he knew of a garage that was open. He didn't, but he assured me that he could find us a place where we could stay overnight and get into a garage in the morning. I told him we had already looked for a room but had been unable to find one. He was so sure he could help us that we got into his car and let him drive us all over town and even some distance up and down the highway.

I managed to be civil to him when it became apparent that he was no more successful than Byrnes had been. He was extremely apologetic. Then he turned the car around and headed for the residential part of town.

"I told you I'd find you a place to stay and I will," he said, smiling over his shoulder. "You'll stay with us tonight! No, it's all right. My wife will be glad to have you. Don't know why I didn't think of it before we did all this chasing around to the motels."

That took the wind out of my sails! I began to feel as

though that horrible day had been worth it if it ended with meeting such Christian people. Sure enough, his wife took us in without blinking an eye—as if she was quite used to having strange people come in after ten o'clock at night to use her guest room.

Lying in bed thinking back on how nasty I had been, I was feeling pretty small. Then I got my comeuppance. From the next room softly muffled through the thin walls, we heard the man praying: "Thank you, God, for sending these lovely people to us."

That broke the ice of meanness that had been imprisoning me all day. I found myself clutching my husband's hand, weeping and apologizing and thanking God all in one breath. For you see, that wonderful man had it all backwards: God hadn't sent us to them—he had sent them to us!

* * *

Actually, Mary is a wonderful person herself. We have only her word for it that she can be as bad-tempered as she paints herself in this story. However, her point is well made. The simple kindness of this man and his wife is a poignant example of the Christian "good neighbor policy" in action.

Acts of simple human kindness often are not glamorous or exciting, yet they give more warmth and happiness than many publicized services. Most of us have at least one friend who always seems to be in the right place at the right time with the right word or the right deed to lighten someone's load. This kind of person is the first to depreciate the value of his or her service, but others recognize its true worth. It takes a special kind of seeing eye and feeling heart to respond to everyday opportunities for this type of ministry.

Ruth Smith is such a person. At a church reunion in Indiana her friend June Wright confided:

Ruth will never tell you this, but there is no one in our congregation who helps as many people as she does. The thing is, few ever know about it. For instance, remember last year when Dave took that business trip to Texas and I wanted to go with him? I hadn't been feeling well and the kids were getting on my nerves something fierce, and I was ready to start climbing the walls. Well, Ruth came over and told me, "Pack up some clothes for the kids. I'm going to keep them while you go to Texas with Dave." She didn't ask me if I wanted her to keep them; she just told me that's how it was going to be. Well, she did keep them, and I did go to Texas with Dave, and I never had such a wonderful trip in my life.

Another thing . . . I found this out by accident because she'd never tell it to anybody . . . she had a neighbor Myrna who had to go into the hospital for several days, and Ruth kept her children for her. She keeps them when Myrna has a doctor's appointment. And there is an elderly lady who isn't too well and her house gets in quite a mess. Know who organizes a mop-and-bucket brigade to tidy things up? Ruth, that's who. She has this knack of seeing the things people need that the rest of us don't notice at all, and she just quietly goes ahead and does something about it.

* * *

Another elderly lady is recipient of neighborly service from Charlotte and Carl Brooks who supply transportation for her whenever she has to go to the hospital or to doctor's appointments. Carl also drives to her house on the first Sunday of each month to take the Communion bread and wine to her. Other members of her church visit her as often as they can to alleviate her loneliness, and all who do testify that they are blessed . . . they receive more than they give. In return the elderly lady is pleased beyond expression when-

51

ever she can do a favor for these friends by baby-sitting when an emergency arises.

[6] Cora Stubbs, another good neighbor, is a middle-aged seamstress in Aurora, Illinois. On May 26, 1968, a group of college students in nearby Wheaton were planning a sympathy demonstration to coincide with the Poor People's March to Washington, D.C. Young people often stopped by Cora's downtown seamstress shop just to talk, so it was natural that they would discuss their plans with her. Since so many demonstrations had ended in violence, Cora suggested that the students might try doing something more constructive than marching. "Let's find ten families in town who need help and do what we can for them," she said. The idea worked so well that Project Love was born and has become a continuing program instead of a one-time-only emergency measure.

Cora has helped quell violence in the ghettos of Chicago, assisted people in finding jobs, and served as a listening post for anyone with a problem. Because of her wide experience she is often asked to lecture. She is also writing a book in which she hopes to share her message of purposeful living, peaceful coexistence, and concern. To her work she brings an abundance of understanding and empathy. She says, "I love people. When they cry, I cry . . . because I know something hurts."

[12] Some good neighbor services require preparation on our part so that we are ready when the necessity arises. According to the president of the St. John Ambulance organization in Canada, half of that country's car crash victims in 1971 who died in the hospital or on the way would have had a good chance of survival if proper first aid had been rendered at the scene of the accident. To reduce

these deaths, he suggests that drivers be required to pass a first aid test before licenses are granted to them and that they also be required to carry first aid kits in their cars. (West Germany already has such a requirement.)

One way we can be good neighbors is to voluntarily take a first aid course. The Red Cross in almost any urban community offers such a course which usually takes three months of one or two evening classes a week. The course, which is free, could come in handy on various occasions. No one knows when a freak accident might happen right before his eyes, and a knowledge of first aid could save a life.

Some good neighbor services require no more preparation. Jan Morris, a Missouri good neighbor, has recorded one of her experiences:

I was driving to Independence on a very hot day, and I was in a hurry. As I drove past a little old lady I recognized her as one who had helped us with vacation church school. She was walking slowly and something inside me said, "Go back and give her a ride."

Since I was rushed I thought, Oh, no, that's just my imagination. She's out walking and really doesn't want a ride. Besides, I'm on a one-way street, and if I go back I'll have to drive around several blocks. That will take a long time, and she isn't going to want a ride anyway! I kept trying to talk myself out of it, but the impulse to pick her up remained.

So I turned around, drove the four blocks that let me get back on this one-way street, and when I got back to the place where I had seen her, she was gone. "Aha," I said to myself, "it *was* all imagination!" But as I started to drive on by I saw that she had walked across the grass and was leaning against a tree. I stopped and asked if she would like a ride. She smiled, nodded, and came over to the car very slowly.

As she got in she told me, "I was asking God to send me a ride. I was telling him that I wasn't complaining because I'm able to walk better than a lot of people I know. I really didn't have enough strength to walk on by myself, so I asked if he would please send somebody to help me. When you stopped, I knew that God had sent you."

I was glad that I hadn't talked myself out of being the one to supply the answer to this good woman's prayer.

* * *

The Lord set the precedent for extending the hand of friendship to those in prison when he said, "I was in prison and ye visited me. . . . Inasmuch as you did it unto one of the least of these my brethren, ye have done it unto me."

* * *

[13] Early in 1953 I had the last of a series of back operations. During my convalescence I thought of my Lord and wondered how I could serve him better than I had been. As a full-time minister I was beginning to feel trapped in what people expected me to do. When I was physically able I preached; I held small group meetings; I visited the sick. People expected me to do this, but my soul seemed to cry out for some means of expression by which I could serve the Lord just because I loved him rather than because of what people expected of me.

In the last days of my convalescence I received a telephone call from the chaplain at the Illinois State Penitentiary in Statesville. He asked if I would come and talk to a young prisoner at the institution. I consented to do so, but on my way to the penitentiary I wondered why he had called me. Since the prisoner did not belong to my church I knew there were literally hundreds of ministers who would be available. Then the car filled with what I recognized as the warmth of God's Spirit, and I knew that here was an answer to my prayers.

At the penitentiary I found I could speak easily with those who are incarcerated. I met the warden, and he asked me to counsel some of the inmates.

When we moved from Aurora to Des Moines, Iowa, I had opportunity to give ministry at Mitchellville, Iowa, the state institution for young women, and at the Iowa State Penitentiary in Fort Madison. Since then I have ministered to prisoners at Marion, Illinois; Menard, Illinois; and Lansing, Kansas; and it has been my privilege to visit on a more or less regular basis at the Federal Penitentiary in Leavenworth, Kansas.

At Leavenworth I became acquainted with three chaplains, four wardens, and hundreds of inmates. One illustration should suffice to tell of the joy of this special ministry. Early in my experience I met a man who long had been in prison (he had spent twenty years in Alcatraz before being transferred to Leavenworth). He was with the gangs of the early thirties and was one newspaper reporters had called "notorious."

Through the years, we developed a strong friendship which has persisted to this day. At the time of our first meeting there seemed to be no possibility of parole because of the sentence he was serving. Through the years, however, he never became discouraged, and his personality blossomed to the point that he was an inspiration to other inmates in the institution. Judges, lawyers, a Catholic chaplain, and I wrote recommending his parole. Finally in October 1966 I came home one day and found my daughter at the doorstep with a letter in her hand. She said, "Hurry, Daddy—it's from Uncle Johnny." I opened the letter and the words seemed to leap from the paper as they told me of his coming release and asked if I could pick him up. On October 31 my son, a friend, and I went to the institution to pick up Uncle Johnny, as he had long been known by my children. Since that time he has led a model life, has been an inspiration to young men in a school where he has worked, has attended reunion with me where he immediately became an inspiration to the young people, and often has had his vacations with us so that indeed he is one of our family.

There have been heartaches because some whom we had hoped to help proved to be beyond our reach. However, the ones like Uncle Johnny have made all of the ministry worthwhile and indeed have verified the experience had on the road to Joliet so many years ago.

The Gideon Society does much more than just place Bibles in hotel rooms around the world although this in itself is a service. Gideons in Terre Haute, Indiana, conduct a weekly Bible study and prayer meeting at the nearby federal penitentiary. Led by a local businessman, James Kline, the project has expanded to include ministers and laymen of many denominations. As so often happens in service of this sort, these men testify that they receive much more than they can possibly give.

Prisoners in another Indiana prison receive a different type of service from an artist who has obtained permission to visit on a regular basis to conduct art classes for the inmates. Neither the prison nor the government could provide funds to help buy supplies, so the artist has been furnishing what he can from his own studio. A few friends, learning of his project, have donated money occasionally, but in general the amount of materials needed is beyond his ability to buy. There is never enough canvas, brushes, or paints to supply the number of prisoners who crowd the art classes. Even so, some superior work has been accomplished, and several paintings have been sold. The prisoners, of course, welcome the chance to earn money in this way to have available when they are released. They welcome, too, the feeling of success and worth which their newfound talent gives them.

* * *

Not everyone has the opportunity to be neighborly to people from a foreign culture. Those who do usually find it an exciting and rewarding adventure in friendship.

* * *

[14] Our introduction to vastly different mores came when we entertained an official representative of the Indonesian government. This was his first experience in an American home, and he was our first Indonesian guest. He was both appalled and fascinated when my husband broiled the steaks for our evening meal. A man cooking was unheard of in his country. His big concern at that time was whether or not to follow his father-in-law's advice to take a second wife.

Probably our most involved volunteer assignment began a few years ago in Topeka, Kansas, with a phone call from a social worker who asked if we would have the time to befriend a young Turkish couple, Bedriye and Remzi Teckgucu. She told that Remzi had been in the States for a couple of years. After graduation from the American University in Istanbul, he had come to the Kansas State University to get a master's degree in engineering. His wife had just recently arrived from Turkey and spoke very little English. Unfortunately, several people had been rather unkind to this young couple whose ways seemed so different from theirs.

The afternoon I stood knocking at the door of their apartment I wondered how I was going to have even a simple conversation, let alone become a friend, if this young woman and I could not understand one another. But I needn't have worried, for with much sign language and a few English words Bedriye had learned from her hours of watching TV, we were able to communicate friendship. She showed me pictures of her family in Turkey, and I in turn pulled out my billfold to show her pictures of my family. She also brought out beautiful pieces of handwork she had made. Later I learned that she had been graduated from a fine girls' school in Turkey where this type of skill is taught.

That evening when my husband came home I told him about the experience I had enjoyed with this young Turkish woman. The more we talked about it the more we felt we should go see both Bedriye and Remzi to extend the hand of friendship from couple to couple. Since they had no phone, we could not call them before going to their apartment. When we arrived, their joy was so great and so genuine we were almost embarrassed. Remzi, who spoke fairly good English, told us that when he had come home that evening Bedriye had told him about this "nice American lady" who had come to visit her. She had shown this lady pictures of their family in Turkey and the American lady had shown her pictures of her American family. Remzi said he knew then that the months of loneliness had become too much for Bedriye, because there was no such thing as a *nice* American lady.

That evening was the beginning of a friendship that has continued through the years and across the miles. Bedriye and I spent many happy hours together while we lived nearby. She picked up the English language very quickly and soon had less of an accent than Remzi. They also began attending church with us occasionally; this was a new experience for us as well as for them, for Bedriye and Remzi were Moslem.

We learned a great deal about these young people who had been shunned by their neighbors because they were different. We learned that Remzi spoke Turkish, English, Greek, and French, and had a reading understanding of several other languages. Bedriye, a well-educated Turkish woman, had a brother who was a government official. Remzi's family apparently was very successful in several business ventures. These were cultured, refined, well-educated people, but they were different—at least different from men and women reared in the United States.

Bedriye was a beautiful woman with thick black hair, sultry blue eyes, and a fair complexion. Remzi was swarthier—typical of the area of Turkey he was from. Their relationship, when we first met them, was a very confining one for Bedriye. Several times when the four of us would be together, Remzi would stop Bedriye from speaking by saying, "Be still, woman." And Bedriye would be still. But time went on, and Bedriye became more independent. One evening Remzi turned to me and said, "Bedriye has changed, and it's all your fault." Thank goodness he was laughing when he made that statement, for she had changed.

Bedriye and Remzi continued going to special church meetings with us. Over and over they told us how much they appreciated the friendship of the church people and they wanted us to know that when they returned to Turkey we or any of our church friends would be welcome in their home. Remzi said it was not the way of his people to welcome strangers, but any friend of ours would not be treated as stranger.

Eventually we all moved from Topeka. About six years later, when the Teckgucus were living in New York and we were living in Connecticut, we visited them one more time. It was a warm summer evening, and they asked if we would like something cool to drink. We said yes, and a few minutes later Remzi appeared from the kitchen with four tall glasses of lemonade. Bedriye gave me a special glance as she accepted a glass from her husband, and Remzi winked when he handed me mine. This was certainly different from the man who a few years before had said, "Be still, woman."

Bedriye and Remzi are now living in Turkey. With each letter they ask when we or our friends are coming to see them. Although they are still Moslem, they think of Christians and particularly our church people with great affection. And we are grateful for the added richness that has been brought into our lives because of our friendship with them. We are also grateful for the opportunity that was ours to make two more friends for Christ.

Mutual friends introduced Luke and Esther Butler to a young Chinese couple from Taiwan. Lawrence and Teresa—students at Indiana State University—were bewildered by American customs, turned off by American food, and lonely in the hustle and bustle of a large American campus. The Butlers opened their home to this young couple, and a friendship developed that extended across the years as Lawrence finished his undergraduate and graduate studies. Teresa taught Esther to cook genuine Chinese food—not chop suey—and Esther "mothered" Teresa, even to the point of mediating an occasional tiff. When Teresa's father visited from Taiwan he brought gifts not only to his daughter and son-in-law but also to their "American parents." When Lawrence and Teresa decided to remain in the United States, it was, naturally enough, the Butlers who acted as their sponsors by signing legal papers promising to assume financial responsibility for them if such ever became necessary. "They are fine young people," say the Butlers. "We are proud to be their friends. They have much to give wherever they go." The

Butlers have a great deal to give, also, and they give it generously as good neighbors wherever they are.

* * *

Mary and Byrnes Fleuty know how to be on the giving as well as the receiving end of "good neighborship."

A friend of ours wrote and said that a Korean nurse had just arrived at the Mississauga Hospital. . . . She was lonely and didn't speak much English. . . . Would we please go and call on her?

We invited her to come to dinner and since she was a Christian, we asked her to attend our study group meeting on Thursday night. This was in January of 1967. Kaja came out often to our home after that, and we helped her learn English. She was a clever girl and caught on quickly. (Actually, she wasn't a student nurse. She had taken her training in Korea, but she had to study in a Canadian hospital for two years and take the R.N. examination before she could be licensed.)

A month after we met Kaja, Byrnes had a serious heart attack. By good luck (or perhaps by divine intervention) he got on Kaja's floor. Her prayers and the devoted care she gave him (nothing was too good for "Daddy" as she called him) helped him to recover.

In April he was back in the hospital with his second heart attack, and again Kaja cared for him. He was still convalescing on our wedding anniversary, and Kaja and Nancy Chang (another Korean who had also joined our "family" by then) arranged a surprise for us. They got permission to prepare and serve a celebration supper in the hospital room. They set up and decorated a card table, and Byrnes and I were made to feel like royalty.

Other friends of Kaja and Nancy began to come to Canada to complete their training, and somehow many of them managed to end up in Mississauga. When we would get word that they were arriving, Kaja and I would meet them at the Toronto airport and take them to the hospital where they were assigned. They were wonderful girls, and our home was busy with their comings and goings.

Kaja was a good daughter to her family back in Korea. When she began earning money she always sent some home to her mother to help the family. Even when she married and had children of her own she kept sending money back to her Korean family. We have also had the happiness of helping a little there, too. Kaja asked me once if I knew of anyone who could help her send her cousin through school. Well, of course . . . *we* could! He is in Seoul University now and doing well.

We have had several Korean weddings in our home. We love all the people who have "adopted" us, but Kaja has always been rather special. She was the first, and she is brilliant. Of all the nurses at Mississauga Hospital she was chosen to take a special supervisor's course.

Pardon me if I sound like a proud mother, but that's how I feel. Kaja and her husband—both Christians—have built a homelife to be proud of. They have bought a house and a car, yet—being good stewards—they send money home to her mother in Korea. And they have brought over her sister and brother and helped them get a start here. Why, they have even bought a milk store and set the brother up in business. Not bad for two Koreans who could hardly speak English when they arrived in Toronto in 1967!

* * *

Mary and Byrnes do sound like proud parents when they talk about Kaja and Bob, but don't try to give them any credit for the success story because they won't allow it.

"Kaja and Bob are great young people . . . they did it all themselves," they insist.

Helping foreigners learn the language and customs of their new country can be an individual and very personal experience. It can also be widened and shared by many in an organized situation. Nettie Cook shares this type of experience.

Being next in line at the check-out counter in a Houston supermarket where I frequently shopped, I heard the checker say, "Twelve dollars and fourteen cents, please." She was speaking to a young Oriental mother who was holding a sleeping baby in her arms while another child, about two years old, stood close by holding to his mother's skirt with both hands. The customer looked at the bag of groceries, then back at the cash register figures while searching in her shoulder bag for a ten-dollar bill which she handed to the girl behind the counter. "I'm sorry," replied the checker, "this is not enough," holding out her hand. The young customer smiled when she handed another ten over the counter.

Before walking away, she turned to me and, in her language, said what I believed to be an apology for the delay which she had caused. I felt helpless and awkward because I could not understand her or offer to help her with the children and the groceries. Nevertheless, I smiled and said, "That's okay," at which time she gracefully bowed, facing me. Later I learned that "okay" has the same meaning in Chinese as in English.

My desire to help this young person that morning, while on the way to my church to attend a weekly Woman's Missionary Society meeting, changed the course of my life from one with much leisure time to the busiest four years of my life. My desire also changed the Missionary Society

63

meetings from the boring, praying-for-missionaries-to-do-His-work kind into a school where more than five hundred women from other countries have learned to speak English.

Putting aside my frustration of feeling awkward and helpless, I began to make plans to approach the church group with the idea of organizing English classes to help persons such as this Chinese girl. There were certain obstacles in my mind that would have to be overcome. The "certain obstacles" were prejudices that had been expressed during my seven years of association with the group.

Martha, the president, opened the meeting with a typical prayer asking God to be in our midst. I thought, Yes, we need You today more than ever before. The collection plate was passed for the "love offering" which we had not used for a project in over a year. We were asked to pray in sequence beginning from left to right "asking for guidance to our foreign missionaries." Sitting to the speaker's left, I began, "Our heavenly Father, forgive us for being here hour after hour each week, wasting our time when we should be teaching English to those . . ." and then I portrayed the grocery store incident in the remainder of my prayer.

Adding support to my appeal, others told of similar experiences where a lack of communication due to a language barrier had caused frustration, hardship, and confusion.

The seventeen members voted unanimously to establish a school and begin classes on a person-to-person basis as soon as possible. Our new project was named "Willow Meadows International Neighbors" (W.I.N.).

The soon-as-possible involved four weeks of hard work and planning by the seventeen volunteers. Each day enthusiasm increased, especially in those making personal calls to prospective students. Night visits were more effective because the prospects' husbands could serve as interpreters. In addition to these personal contacts, brochures were posted on bulletin boards in grocery stores and apartment units:

WILLOW MEADOWS INTERNATIONAL NEIGHBORS
(W.I.N.)
9999 Green Willow, Houston, Texas
English lessons (no charge)
private teacher
Nursery provided for children
Transportation—telephone 723-8254
Tuesdays, 9:30-11:30 a.m.
Books—The Dixon Series of
Conversational English
(furnished)

Opening day looked like a little United Nations meeting. Twenty-one girls from eleven countries dressed in their native styles represented the enrollment; sixteen children were cared for in the nursery. The first student enrolled was my friend Shi-Wen Huang (Sue for short) whose husband saw the announcement in the supermarket where we had first met.

Five years later W.I.N. has an average enrollment of one hundred and thirty students representing fifty-four countries.

Sue and other former students have joined the W.I.N. staff of a hundred and eighty volunteers. I believe that while the pupils learn English the American volunteers have experienced something more important—the joy of learning the international language of love.

To meet other community needs members of a group can fan out into many areas of service helping their neighbors as individuals and still come back together to lend each other encouragement and assistance. A group endeavor such as this can strengthen the efforts of the persons involved.

* * *

[15] During the summer months of 1970 various social welfare agencies, the Police Department, parole board, and other groups providing community services sent representatives to discuss their programs at our Orlando church on Sunday evenings. Through them we received firsthand, authoritative information about the urgent human needs around us and were asked to find a program in which we might serve.

We soon had to face a problem shared by members of many urban churches. Where exactly was our "community"? Members of our congregation are scattered over a wide area in several towns and suburbs in four different counties. Was this entire area our community? Or was it the several blocks surrounding the church building itself? Or could the "community" be the location where each church member lived, worked, or attended school?

We also had to consider how much time was required by the members to carry on the worship services and other organized activities of the congregation. We wondered how much of our limited financial resources could be involved in this outreach program. A sum of money was eventually designated for community service in the church budget.

Ultimately, forty-two members decided to investigate participating in some kind of an organized effort to serve human needs. A flexible organization called the D'n'A Club signifying dedication and action was formed. This course of action was chosen because, at the time, it was not possible to select any single project that the congregation as a corporate body would endorse and support.

At the first D'n'A meeting, areas of need in the broad community of the congregation were again emphasized and members were asked to serve in a program of their own choice. The group then decided to meet at the church on the first Friday evening of each month to discuss the previous month's service activities. Those members already engaged in volunteer work were encouraged to continue their activities as "D'n'A" projects. For instance, several women had transcribed religious literature into braille books for the blind for many years.

Four members volunteered to answer telephone calls for "We Care" and the teen-age "Hot Line." These twenty-four-hour services operate in many communities to bring immediate response and aid to desperate people with problems. These volunteers were taught by medical and social welfare personnel.

At least four people began to visit regularly in nursing and extended care homes. Elderly D'n'A-ers decided to go the second mile in helping neighbors with unique problems. Several people volunteered to help "pattern" the muscle and nervous systems of children with physical disabilities. In these instances, time was required each day.

The pastor found that as a minister he had access to the local jails and could visit with prisoners who often only needed to talk with someone from the "outside." Another lay minister worked as a volunteer with the Pardon and Parole Commission rehabilitation program.

Other community services that were aided were the Girl Scouts, Boy Scouts, League of Women Voters, PTAs, a county-wide vision screening program, several school clinics, the "FISH" (Friend, I Seek Help) program, Florida Boys Ranch, Edgewood Boys Ranch, and a high school boys' club. In many instances, leadership for these activities was provided by D'n'A-ers. During this time, an Orlando Branch account was opened at the Central Florida Blood Bank and members were asked to donate the ten pints needed to keep the account current.

As the program evolved, most of us shed some tears and had perplexing moments as we came face-to-face with the needs of others. In some cases we could give little except a listening ear and a word of encouragement. But in others we were surprised at how much our efforts could achieve.

The Orlando Branch is a large church in a large city. However, size is no prerequisite for service. A small church group in a small town can also accomplish great things for the community.

[16] Soldiers Grove, Wisconsin, is a village of 541 people. Our church, located four miles south, has an enrollment of 145 and an average attendance of sixty.

There are twelve teen-agers, nine of whom are active in our young people's group. The League leaders are Dale and Barbara Duke. Dale teaches vocal music in our school system and Barbara is a kindergarten teacher. Under their leadership the Leaguers have reached out to the youth of other faiths—and no faith.

Our vacation church school is also a community project. During the five years that I have taught in it we have had an average attendance of fifty children from various faiths.

Joyce Banta lives in a nearby town and is active in community life there. She has been asked to teach a class in another church on the use of visual aids.

Hazel Crouse, a senior citizen, is community life chairman of our women's department. She is very active in senior citizen activities and for years has used her car to take elderly people to the doctor or shopping or wherever they needed to go. She has another project now—raising African violets for gifts to the sick. I have been with her and have seen the joy these violets bring, especially in the people who realize the work behind the gift.

June Rosemeyer is a welcome sight to the older people, particularly when she delivers a freshly cooked meal, which she often does. She also bakes and decorates wedding cakes at a minimal charge. For many brides a cake made by June is part of the wedding tradition. The money she receives from the cakes is her personal contribution to the church building fund.

The people of the Soldiers Grove area raised the necessary funds for a Rescue Van which serves all of northern Crawford County. The Van is manned by volunteer workers who have taken the necessary training. No charge is made for the service, which is maintained by donations. Last winter the women's department under the leadership of Lana Olson served a supper at the Legion Hall for the benefit of the Rescue Squad (it was quite successful).

Two years ago members of a homemakers' group in the Yankestown community decided they would like to start a library in Soldiers Grove. The village board was quite helpful, providing the necessary quarters and the materials needed. I am interested in reading and libraries so I volunteered to help. Thanks to publicity in the local papers, we received books from as far away as California. I helped process the books and now serve as a volunteer librarian. Four other ladies work as volunteer librarians also; this enables us to keep the library open nineteen hours a week. We soon outgrew the original quarters and the board voted to provide us with permanent quarters. A library board was appointed when the library became state accredited, and I serve as president of the board. We have mostly second-hand books but have been pleased with the quality of books donated. As the library became established, we started to receive memorial funds, with which we have bought new books. Our last year-end inventory showed a count of 4,500 books.

On the opposite side of the country another good neighbor, person-to-person ministry of service was started.

* * *

[17] In May of 1969 a group of twenty-eight church members under the leadership of Neil Simmons established the Amigos Mission in East Los Angeles. This was a storefront mission located in the largest Mexican community outside of Mexico City. The purpose of the mission and its personnel was to provide assistance for the people of the community. A referral service was started to enable them to find help and, hopefully, solutions to many of their problems, such as legal needs, welfare assistance, and immigration difficulties.

We started by forming girls' clubs; these were an instant success. There were so many that our building seemed to bulge at the sides. We discovered that many of these children knew happiness only when they were in the Amigos Center where they could be held, hugged, and loved.

Adults began to call us as they became aware of the service. One of our most ardent supporters and helpers was the man who owned the building and ran a barbershop next door. Leo Escarcega was always eager to translate for us or help by answering the phone. We had only to knock on the wall for immediate response.

We do not know the number of lives in the community that were changed in some way by our presence, but we do know that some of the young people in the local high school were helped. Some of them were granted scholarships to college and still others were able to get jobs as a result of this project. Many have learned to drive autos and secure jobs as a result of assistance received at the Mission. Several are now in the United States legally instead of illegally. Still others have been able to get needed medical help. Some learned that there was a God and that he cared what happened to them. Others found simply that somebody cared.

During the riots that occurred in this area we traveled to and from the Mission without being harmed in any way, and we were able to help calm the fears of some of the children during this terrible time. When a severe earthquake occurred later we again were able to help quell the fears of the children.

An incident that took place during the second year of our operation will perhaps serve as an example of the dramatic results of our service.

On a Thursday morning Leo, our barber friend, called Ron Van Fleet and said that a woman was in desperate need of help. She had been charged with the murder of her husband and was being held at the Sybil Brand Institute for Women. She had been in jail for a week with no legal counsel and had not seen anyone except her sister who was unable to do anything for her.

Ron went immediately to the barbershop to talk to the sister. With Leo's help he pieced together the story. The husband, who had come home from the Korean war two decades before with a mental disorder, had grown worse over the ensuing years. On several occasions he had threatened to kill his wife and/or children. The family lived on welfare, and the wife would have had nowhere to go if she had left him. During one of his periodic spells of irrationality the husband had brought home a gun and threatened the family. When the wife went downstairs the next morning after a sleepless night, she got possession of the gun and killed him. Now she was in Sybil Brand, alone and terrified.

As a minister Ron made arrangements to visit Mrs. Hernandez. They met in the waiting room where attorneys talk to their clients. The noise was quite loud and music played constantly. Against this background Mrs. Hernandez told Ron the whole story again. She had killed her husband because she was afraid for her children and herself. Now she had no idea what would happen to her. Her concern at that time was not for herself but for her children, particularly for her twelve-year-old son who was at a reform school in Ventura, California. Ron assured her that we would contact the school.

Although Mrs. Hernandez was a Roman Catholic, she did not want to see a priest; she was very afraid that she had committed a mortal sin. "I spoke to her of the mercy of Jesus and of his great love for her," Ron recalls. "I told her that although she would always carry the guilt of her act the Lord wanted her to know that he forgave her and would not leave her alone."

After leaving the jail Ron went back to the Amigos Center and started calling attorneys. He started with a private lawyer who had been referred to the Hernandez family. This man said that he would need a minimum retainer of $10,000 to take the case and he would not promise anything. He had read her booking for murder one and felt that the very best he could get her was murder two, and even this would be difficult. Ron thanked him and, after talking again with Leo, called the Public Defender's Office in the city of Los Angeles.

By the following Tuesday Ron had arranged for a public defender to see Mrs. Hernandez and went to see her again himself. He found her in much better spirits. She had seen a man from the Public Defender's Office and agreed to go before the judge for a preliminary hearing to set a trial date on the coming Monday. Again Ron talked to her about the love and forgiveness of Christ and assured her that there would be many prayers in her behalf all that week.

The hearing was set for early Monday morning. By noon Leo was on the phone, almost incoherent with excitement. Mrs. Hernandez was home with her children. The judge, after hearing her case, had declared it justifiable homicide and dismissed the charges against her. He said that justice would be served much better by the mother being home with her children.

As we rejoiced at the news we were reminded of the words of the Master, "When I was in need ye comforted me."

The Amigos Center was formed to serve the souls of people; nothing was asked in return. There were no prices on its services, no religious meetings in payment for assistance, no preaching. Workers at the Center believed that the best message they could give was their lives.

* * *

Perhaps in a way any instance of loving personal service could be called part of the "Good Neighbor Policy." However, there seems to be something special about the people-to-people services described in this chapter. It takes a spontaneous outpouring of love, a thoughtful heart, and quick insight into the needs of another human being to produce this quality of caring.

CHAPTER FOUR

"Of Such Is the Kingdom"

[18] It seems a long time ago that Bob and I began our adventure with children, but in fact it has been only fourteen years. We were both twenty-two years old and trying to farm productively, but working at other jobs to make ends meet. My mother decided she could no longer handle my two younger brothers and sister and asked Bob if they could live on the farm with us while she went to Toronto to work. I wasn't willing, but Bob agreed and because he was the "head of our house" we acquired the first three of our children.

Less than a year later, my sister separated from her husband and asked if we could care for her two girls while she went to work. We agreed to take them for one year. So then there were five: Colleen, twelve; Terry, eleven; Stuart, six; Robin, four; and Susan, one. For the next eight years we were a family involved in church activities—CGIT (Canadian Girls in Training), Tyros, choir, school activities, concerts, plays, music lessons, ball games, gardening, feeding chickens, riding ponies, skating, haying. . . . Then Colleen found Andy and Bob walked down the aisle and gave her away . . . and I cried.

When Robin was twelve, her mother remarried and asked for the girls. During the eight years between, we had gone through many bad experiences with their mother when she would bring one man home and tell the girls he was going to be their new father; then a few weeks later she would bring another man with the same promise. Once she came and took them back to Toronto with her. Three days later they called to say they didn't have anything to eat. In a couple of hours we were knocking at the door of a one-room cabin behind a garage on Dundas Street West. They not only didn't have anything to eat, they hadn't eaten for two days. That was the first and last time they were away from us until their mother started living with a man and brought him and the police to demand the children. She wasn't successful. The girls cried and clung to us, and the police refused to force them. Two months later, after tearful consultations with the Children's Aid, we allowed Robin to go. Susan still refused: Bob and I were the only parents she could remember. Six months passed, and we received the news that there was trouble. My sister had asked the Children's Aid to place Robin in a foster home.

During this time, life had been changing on the home-front, too. Terry was graduated from high school, a shining occasion of success because he was the first of my whole family of ten sisters and four brothers to graduate. I felt it had been worth it all. Now he wanted to farm, and Bob had to make a big decision. We sold our small farm, bought two larger ones, and went into farming (and debt) in earnest.

Then Terry met Margaret, and we knew that before long there would be another empty plate at our ever diminishing table.

At this point Bob and I started to think and pray. We had a big house, plenty of beds, energy, love, and lots of experience . . . maybe we could find some kids who needed us. We called the Children's Aid and asked if there might be any eight- or ten-year-olds who needed a home. We haven't been without a foster child since, but only one of them was ten. The others were and are all teen-agers—mostly boys.

Ken was one of them and came when he was fourteen

years old, on probation for stealing. (He had been in fourteen other foster homes.) He left when he was eighteen, and again I cried. We had had four years of learning to love him. He still comes home, and we miss him when he stays away too long.

He wasn't the only boy in trouble with the law. We have Rick who also was on probation and found it hard adjusting even to us. One night this spring, he came home after a special youth service at the church and solemnly declared, "I have just given my heart and life to Jesus Christ." This from a boy who had run away, experimented with drugs, and destroyed property was pure joy!

But it hasn't all been sweet success; there have been failures too. One was Bert. He was sixteen and had never been taught how to live with other people. He threw his dirty clothes back in his drawer with the clean ones. "Deodorant" was a foreign word—as was "bath." The other children—there were five at the time—resented his ways and I didn't understand him. Finally I asked that he be placed somewhere else. Even now it hurts to write of my failure.

The year after we moved, my sister decided she wanted Susan, too, and during divorce proceedings she applied for custody. Except for the grace of God, she would have been given this custody before we even knew of the hearing. For six months our life was in turmoil with lawyers, witnesses, and even a psychiatrist.

One thing we knew for sure—Susan wanted to stay with us. She was now twelve, doing well in school (almost all A's), and she knew the Lord. We trusted him to guide us, and just before we went to court we asked our lawyer for a few minutes alone. We knelt and prayed that God would have his way in this matter and that we would be willing to accept whatever it was. The judge awarded us complete custody. We were very grateful and still are. We never had any doubts even when our lawyer presented us with the bill . . . $4,281! We know the worth of these children which have been entrusted to us, and it isn't measured in dollars and cents.

* * *

Many people have opened their homes to foster children . . . both orphans and children in trouble with the law. Some of these foster homes—let's face it—are business ventures operated for a profit. But many foster parents are producing miracles every day by giving love along with food and bed.

* * *

[19] The baby the caseworker had brought me was the most pitiful looking thing I had ever seen. She was four months old and had a hole in her heart. Her eyes were glassy, and she showed no emotion at all. Her skin was flaky and had red blotches all over it. She looked as if she had been terribly neglected. I took one look and thought, Oh, my . . . this baby is something else!

So naturally we took little Angela into our hearts and loved the daylights out of her.

A week later the caseworker came back to pick up another baby we were keeping. When she came in we had Angela in her infant seat on the davenport. The caseworker walked by her and said, "Here's a cutie. Whose baby is this?"

I said, "That's the one you brought me last week."

"What?" She went back to take another look. "I can't believe it's the same child."

Being with her all the time I hadn't noticed how much she had changed. She was gooing and smiling, her eyes were bright and snappy, and all of the eczema on her skin had gone away. Now she was soft and cuddly and alert.

And I thought to myself, This is what it's all about. . . .

One week of love had changed this baby into a happy, beautiful child.

* * *

Sometimes a family tragedy opens up the need for this kind of service. This happened to Rowena whose sister-in-law died four days after giving birth to a son. When the baby was released from the hospital, Rowena and her husband took him home along with their own four children. Their youngest was hardly more than a baby, so it was like looking after twins. The Hamiltons kept their little nephew for two-and-one-half years until his father remarried. Even today he seems like one of their own and holds a special place in their hearts.

Another foster mother, Adeline E. Judd of Ontario, made this comment about foster parenthood: "We have had many lovely experiences with these children. We have taken them to the lake, gone swimming with them, played with them, and had great fun. We have tried to teach them about the Lord Jesus Christ and his ways, and we hope that we have found and helped them to find Jesus. For us this has been a very worthwhile venture in applied Christianity."

Perhaps that is a good definition of service: applied Christianity.

Various juvenile courts are experimenting with other methods of dealing with delinquent children. One community in Ontario has established "Opportunity House." The house parents are, of course, a married couple—preferably with children of their own. They must have large quantities of patience and be able to establish good rapport with boys who may be hostile and uncooperative. The boys, referred by the courts, are fourteen to sixteen years old and come from all kinds of home situations. Opportunity House (and there may be several households operating under this name in one general location) will take no more than four boys into any one home so that the family group will be small enough to permit a great deal of loving personal interaction. Every attempt is made to effect a close approximation of a real family. Although the boys may have been classed as incorrigible by the courts, they attend regular schools and are allowed to go out at night. There must be some rules, of course, just as any family must have. The boys must, for instance, be in the house by curfew time, and they are on their honor to "keep the peace." Being house parents for Opportunity House may be considered a job, but it takes a special kind of people dedicated to lives of service to act as father and mother to incorrigible delinquents.

Churches and social service centers in large cities are also sponsoring coffeehouses and youth clubs. One such is the Drop-In Center in Rochester, New York.

* * *

One day four years ago Dr. Ray Fedje was about to enter the large church of which he was pastor when he noticed a group of boys throwing rocks at pigeons. The pigeons were getting the worst of it and the stained-glass windows of the church seemed in imminent danger too, when the minister decided to see if he could stop it. Talking with the boys he found that all of them lived in the neighborhood and had nothing to do except roam the streets looking for trouble or entertainment.

Dr. Fedje again started to his office, but something took him to the basement of the house next door which was also owned by the church. The basement was big with rambling coal bins encrusted with years of dust. As he stood there an idea began to take shape in his mind. Back out in the street he got several boys to go with him to look at the basement, and as they walked through it he said casually, "How about fixing this place up with a pool table and some ping-pong tables? Are you interested?"

Skeptical at first, they became enthusiastic when they learned that the place would be for them alone, not the "dudes" who were the regular parishioners. Dr. Fedje took his plan to the church board, and money was appropriated to install plumbing and heating and make necessary structural changes. What the neighborhood kids could do themselves, they did. As they worked Dr. Fedje became "Doc," and they became "Fedje's Gang."

The Drop-In Center was open every evening, with one night a week reserved for a special coffeehouse atmosphere. Some of the gang had formed a group called the Golden Links, and that was their night to take over. Another night was open only to older teen-agers. The remaining nights were for anyone who wanted to "drop in".

The church, a cathedral-type edifice located downtown with inner city residential area around it, has a large congregation made up largely of parishioners from the well-groomed suburbs. The young people who are regular members of the church do not participate in the Drop-In activities, although there has been some attempt to integrate them with Fedje's Gang in summer activities when they have held swim parties at their home pools.

A few of the parishioners are still uptight about the grubby neighborhood teen-agers who occasionally come to Sunday morning church and greet their minister at the door by throwing their arms around him. The integrated swim parties have not been a complete success, either. After one of them an irate mother told Dr. Fedje that one of his gang had blackened her son's eye. She did not know the reason for the scuffle, and her son would not tell. When Doc asked the offender, he bristled and charged, "He called me a bastard. Nobody can do that and get away with it."

"Most of my gang would only laugh if somebody called them that," Dr. Fedje explained, "but you see, this boy *is* a bastard, and that makes all the difference in the world. His friends in the neighborhood know it and they don't mention it."

In the evening when he drives home from the church Doc never takes the most direct route, but crisscrosses the neighborhood "looking after his kids." One night following a meeting that ended about ten p.m., a group of boys spotted him and flagged him down. "Wally's dropped acid in my bedroom, and I'm scared. I gotta get rid of him, man, but I don't know what to do." Doc took Wally back to the church and put him on a couch in the office. At midnight Wally's mother called because somebody had said he was with Doc. "I'll have him home to you, but I don't know how soon," Dr. Fedje told her.

Wally spent most of that night in the church office until he slept off the acid and could be taken home. Later he asked, "Doc, why do you go on doing things for us kids when we mess around and keep you all screwed up?"

"I don't approve of some of the things you do, but I never stop loving you."

Wally stared at him. "Well, I'll be damned!" he muttered. "I just don't understand."

Doc smiled. "I don't expect you to, but someday you will."

Craig is another member of the gang who feels Doc's love but doesn't understand it. Recently while he was in jail for burglary Doc was a frequent visitor. He wrote a letter trying to say what he felt: "When I get out of this mess and get my own pad and car, I'll come and take care of you. . . . There are only two people in all the world I can count on to love me. My mother and you." Coming from Craig, that was quite a compliment.

The boys in Fedje's Gang do not use language for the squeamish. "They don't clean it up for me either," says Doc, "and that's good. They know they don't have to put on a front. They let me see them as they are, and that lets me get closer to them than other people can." It also gives him opportunities to help them that other people never have.

One day Wally used such foul language that Doc finally said, "Wally, can't you find any better way to express yourself?"

Wally stuck out his chin. "Who's going to teach me?" he challenged.

Doc blinked but came back with an answer. "I will."

A few days later Wally was in the church office when a man came in to see Dr. Fedje. He introduced the man and boy. Wally mumbled "Hi" but didn't move from his chair. When the man left, Doc said, "You know, Wally, when you are introduced to an adult you should stand up, go over to him, hold out your hand and say, 'How do you do, Mr. Davis? I'm glad to meet you.' "

"Aw, no, Doc. None of that crap for me."

"Well, Wally, you said you wanted to learn how to talk and act. I'm just trying to teach you."

The next time Wally was in the office another man came in. Again Dr. Fedje performed the introduction. This time Wally got up, walked across the room, poked out his hand to the man, and all in one breath said, "How do you do Mr. Smith I'm glad to see you how's that Doc?"

Dr. Fedje's eyes soften as he talks about his Gang.

"We're making some changes this fall. . . . We're going to have a day care center for working parents who don't know what to do with their kids when they come home from school and nobody is back from work yet. And we're going to have a coffeehouse every night to replace the old Drop-In. I think it will be better for them now."

A young person doesn't have to be an orphan or in trouble with the law to need help. Sandy recently lost his father. A teen-ager, Sandy is insecure, lonely, often bewildered because he has no father figure to turn to. At a Christian Aschram in Ontario he met Brother Ray, a busy minister of a large metropolitan church. Brother Ray took him "under his wing," but his interest in the boy's needs did not end with that weekend—just as Sandy's needs did not end with that weekend. Although he lives a hundred miles from Sandy's home, he has kept in regular contact, writing him frequent letters even when Sandy doesn't write back. While Sandy was in a boarding school Brother Ray visited him every month and called him on the telephone just to let him know somebody still cared. This past summer, he took the boy to another Aschram, acting as his sponsor and friend. Sandy's family loves him, but Brother Ray answers a need in his life that no one else is filling right now: a father figure, a guide, an anchor in time of trouble.

Brother Ray, with a daughter but no sons, seems to have an affinity for disturbed and frightened boys. Another of his "adopted sons" is a Jewish boy whose parents are divorced. The situation has left David unhappy, lonely, and confused. Brother Ray has spent many hours with this boy, taking him on outings around the city, planning and sharing activities, or just talking with him about his problems. David knows that he can call on him for help at any time. One night David did put in a collect call and in a scared, shaking voice said, "Papa, I need you." He and another boy, both twelve years old, had run away from home that day. When they found themselves miles away from the city late at night with no place to stay, soaking wet from a storm, hungry and without money, they called the only man they knew who could be trusted to give them help. Brother Ray drove across the city to get them, took them to his home, dried their clothes, fed them, and talked with them until four o'clock in the morning. Finally, the boys became convinced that running away was not the answer to their problems. The only solution was learning to face difficulties. For them that meant letting Brother Ray drive them home so they could explain their actions and feelings to their families and try to "talk their problems out."

Leaders of church youth groups have a special field of service open to them which can be immensely challenging and rewarding. The youth leaders of Soldiers Grove, Wisconsin, in addition to the regular meetings and established programs, have taken their teen-agers to youth camps, retreats, skating parties, and bowling. On recent "Float-In's" they drove the young people upriver with rafts, supervised floating downstream to Soldiers Grove, picked them up again, and took them home.

After evening meetings or projects, the young people were always hungry, but the only place open to get something to eat late at night was the tavern—clearly not the place to take a group of church young people. The Dukes felt there was only one answer: "Come on over to our house. We always have something we can snack on." So it became established procedure to end an evening at their home with pizzas, hamburgers, and pop. The story might have ended there if the young people hadn't been having so much fun that they began bringing other friends in town. It wasn't long until there were more kids than the Duke house could hold. Fortunately at this point the town got interested and provided a hall for the young people to use for their meetings and parties. Dale and Barbara were still the leaders, and the Leaguers helped staff the projects and parties which took place there. Later when the townspeople became concerned about doing something for the young adults and senior citizens of their community the remark was heard, "Well, we

84

don't have to worry about doing something for our young people. They're already provided for."

Another church youth group in Australia ran into some interesting problems in trying to assimilate "outlanders" into the ranks.

[20] A few years ago the youth group in our congregation underwent rather a striking change. Up until that time it had consisted of young members of the church, with perhaps an occasional friend or two taking part, and it had always been relatively small. However, when the new group of church youth reached League age an interesting thing happened. Some of them already belonged to a group—one of those unorganized but vigorous collections of young people who live in the same district and move around together—and before we knew what had happened they were all attending League. What's more, it wasn't long before they brought others, and suddenly we found our League had swelled to fifty. This sounds like a situation to delight any congregation—particularly one whose League had usually numbered about ten—but unfortunately it created a number of difficulties.

To start with, the new members—nearly all boys—were what might be called the "unchurched." In clothing, grooming, speech, and life-style they were very different from the young people most of the leaders were accustomed to. We were anxious to make some contribution to their lives that would be significant but were uncertain how best to do it. First we found it necessary to undertake an immediate revision of our program. Activities and studies suited to the church group no longer seemed adequate to meet the needs of these newcomers. We had to consider what could be done that would be of help to both member and nonmember and make an effort to implement this as quickly as possible.

Control also became a problem. We had never had any need for rules before. Now we found that very early in our association we had to establish stipulations about conduct. Extra supervision was needed to enforce some of them. The boys were energetic and noisy. They were not used to respecting any property—much less the sanctity of the chapel. One group sent into the church proper in the course of a discussion session was found sitting in the baptismal font smoking.

We had to think through our attitudes toward incidents like this. Many of us wondered if we could handle the situation. Some in the congregation asked whether we should. Did we really want these people in our League? One or two might have been absorbed, but there were so many that they far outnumbered the member Leaguers. Could we influence them, or would it be the other way around? Would we achieve anything? And we had to look at our deep-seated attitudes too. Did we feel superior? Were we patronizing? Did we think that we were doing them a favor by allowing them in our League? Was it too easy to look at them as "different," less "worthwhile"?

With these questions continuing to occupy our minds, we set out to do all we could to make our activities meaningful in the lives of the boys. Most of them did not have stable homes, the benefit of friendly advice from adults who cared about them, a knowledge of some of the basic facts about adult life without which so many pitfalls can arise, or the help of anyone when things went wrong. Some of these lacks we felt we could begin to supply. Some of our earliest experiences with these youth included appearing with them in Juvenile Court, speaking for them and offering what help we could. This, more than anything else, began to create a warm relationship; they began to trust us, and we began to understand them a little more.

Because of their background and brushes with authority, they had an attitude toward law which was a mixture of defiance, mistrust, and dislike. So one of the first meetings—and indeed one of our most successful—featured a friend of ours, a magistrate, as speaker. This young man in his early thirties was still able to talk the language of youth and related particularly well to the boys. He talked to them about the law in general, how it came to be the way it was, and why it was important in the community. Then he answered questions; they came slowly at first, but then nearly everyone in the group began talking at once. His approachable manner and his willingness to answer even those questions which were aggressively shouted obviously impressed his audience. A little later we asked a young policeman to be the guest speaker. Those who had had experiences with angry and sometimes unpleasant members of the force were inclined to be suspicious of him at first, but as he talked—ostensibly about safe driving, the best way to avoid accidents, and how to care for vehicles—they became responsive and were soon asking him questions on all sorts of problems. Again a good relationship developed, and a certain modifying of their attitudes was obvious.

All of the group had left school, but none of them had good jobs and several were unemployed. Financial matters were of importance to them, and one evening a member who was experienced in financial counseling came to talk. His approach too was excellent; he couched his comments in their terms and realistically dealt with their problems—the dangers of hire purchase, the results of mounting unpaid bills, the value of making at least a rudimentary budget. Again they listened and asked questions. What he said interested them and made sense.

On another occasion we asked a member who was a trained social worker to discuss with them social pressures, advertising, and the manipulation of groups by the mass communication media. The boys were obviously surprised and impressed by some of the facts they were not aware of before.

We are fortunate in our congregation to have two doctors—both women. The first came one evening to talk about health in general, but questions asked led to quite an informative discussion about drugs. The group appreciated the fact that the speaker discussed the subject nonjudgmentally and unemotionally, giving the facts simply as she saw them and answering questions honestly. The other, at another time, came to talk about abortion. The subject was in the forefront of the news at the time, and all of the young people were interested in it. Again with every effort not to judge or moralize the speaker discussed what abortion was and some of the reasons for and against it. In the process she sparked a discussion on a whole range of sexual matters; it continued far beyond the normal meeting time. The level of participation was high, and at the end of the evening they did not need to express in words how much the discussion had meant to them.

Sometimes we talked on issues of more depth—about the future, the meaning of life, what values were important. Often we led into this by discussing the lyrics of popular songs. We were always gratified at how well they responded—not in the way we would have, and not always with ideas that we could commend, but at least with honesty. We learned a lot about one another in these discussions.

In cooperation with the education section of the Marriage Guidance Council we organized a series of meetings on self-understanding and interpersonal relationships. Held on a Sunday evening, these were surprisingly well attended. Counselors and discussion leaders from the council came to lead groups and stimulate discussion; again these youth surprised us by their freely expressed—though often un-orthodox—views. Valuable material on self-discovery, self-development, relationships with parents, spouses, and society in general was presented.

Of course such meetings were not held every week. They had to be interspersed among more vigorous activities. Some service projects met with success despite our initial doubts. Several of the boys liked to play together as a group, and although the music was not to our taste (and I suspect was not very good in its own idiom either) it proved popular at various institutions which we visited. One that invited us back several times was a training center for delinquent boys. To them our group had tremendous appeal. On several occasions we also entertained mentally retarded teen-agers from a local institution.

Purely social outings were the most popular. Barbecues, hikes, beach parties, swimming, and visits to places of interest were always well attended. Eventually some of the boys formed a basketball team under the direction of our young pastor, a top-grade basketball player himself. This group is still playing and has won several championships. Perhaps even more important was the development of a team spirit which would once have seemed out of the question.

If at times our frequent social outings made it seem that we were only providing entertainment for the group, which would have been available elsewhere, we reminded ourselves that after all the boys had not had it in just this way before. Their amusements had often been of a less desirable kind. The local police made a special point of telling us after the group had been active for a year or so that the level of petty crime, fighting, and vandalism in the neighborhood had fallen quite markedly.

Although to write about the program now makes it seem well planned, interesting, and successful there were times when we felt that it was in fact none of these things. There were many problems, many failures, and constant soul-searching on our part. Even now, when almost all of the boys have drifted away, it is hard to appraise the project. The sort of results we were hoping for, of course, were not the ones that are readily measurable—but we ourselves gained a great deal. Over the four years or so that they stayed with us, our early attitudes of apprehension and reluctance turned into growing friendship and appreciation for a different and rewarding relationship. We came to understand another life-style. We learned at first hand how wrong it is to judge from outward appearances alone. And we discovered the pleasure to be had from serving, from helping youth to develop the potential within them, from enabling others to live more freely and effectively. Trying to help the group do these things seemed to us a worthwhile, Christian task. We can only hope that in this we were at least partially successful.

It's no fun to be on the outside looking in, especially for children. One summer during youth camp at Racine, Missouri, the campers and their director, Ralph Williston, became aware of solemn faces staring over the fence at the good times going on inside the camp. Their hearts were touched by the poverty and wistfulness of these neighborhood children, and they determined somehow to give them a camp of their own.

They began by having camp-for-a-day for some Indian children who lived nearby and then expanded it to a full week of day camping for the disadvantaged in the surrounding area. The camp has grown every year. Similar camps in other places take the underprivileged or the retarded or the crippled. At Racine all three are accepted. Caring for so many needs is made possible only by the assistance of camper helpers on a one-to-one basis. By 1973 there were eighty campers and eighty helpers, plus cooks, instructors, and other staff members. The helpers were young people of senior high and college age from various churches in the Racine area.

A wide variety of activities was provided and the campers could choose what they wanted to do and register for those classes. Included was singing at the morning Hootenany, archery, swimming, music (learning to play the guitar and ukelele), and crafts such as soap carving, artex painting, and making lanyards and collages. There was even a zoo where the children could pet goats, rabbits, dogs, cats, hamsters, and sheep. No one was pushed to attend these activities. The mentally retarded, for example, did what they could with the aid of their camper helper. Some of the more emotionally uncontrolled children simply wandered around doing whatever appealed to them under the supervision and protection of those assigned to them. In case of accidents there were five registered nurses on the grounds. They carried walkie-talkies so they could be called with some privacy when needed. In previous years it had been found that emotionally disturbed children became very upset when they heard the nurses called over the loudspeaker system.

During the week the campers had one overnight at the camp. Each brought his own bedroll and stayed in the cabin with his camper-helper. For many of the children this was the biggest and most exciting adventure of the week.

A feature of the camp is the Storehouse where donated clothing and shoes are kept to be given away as needs arise. State law requires that the children wear shoes, but some of them do not own shoes. They are taken to the Storehouse and outfitted as soon as they arrive in camp so that they don't miss any of the activities. On Wednesday the parents are invited to attend the camp to see what their children are doing and are given the opportunity to buy whatever they need at the Storehouse for five or ten cents an article.

Money to finance the camp comes from many sources. Donations come from individuals, church congregations, clubs, and local businesses. In addition the camper helpers pay their own expenses as well as giving their services. It does take both money and hard work to run the camp, but all who are involved feel that they are more than repaid by the happy faces of the young campers.

* * *

Almost every church operates a vacation Bible school for a week or ten days each summer, but in Canada this is supplemented by the Ontario Children's Fellowship. OCF is an interdenominational club which goes into a neighborhood and organizes an indoor program similar to Bible school. The actual program lasts one week and then moves on into another community. OCF operates all summer, moving from one neighborhood to another through a city. It is particularly welcome in a situation where there is no neighborhood church to conduct Bible schools.

Lindell Gough originated two programs for children which could be used in any community where there are enough people who care.

My work with children actually started when I was a teen-ager and someone asked me to teach the kindergarten class in our church school. Obviously I wasn't qualified, but I dedicated my life to God in this service if he could use me. Later I went to college and earned my degree in elementary teaching.

My years of teaching convinced me that if we were to overcome prejudice and many emotional and mental problems, we would have to start long before children were in kindergarten. One Sunday morning during the spring of 1968 as I sat in church school I decided to quit just talking about it and *do* something. Since my work would be from the convictions of my heart, I decided the name "Heart's Nudge" would be appropriate. The youth of the church agreed to support me, and we immediately began making plans.

Our first program was a three-week session . . . one week in three different schools working with preschool children of welfare families. The superintendent of schools must have been impressed because he requested that we continue Heart's Nudge on a monthly basis during the next school year. As a companion program the church women met with the mothers of these preschool children to discuss dental health, nutrition, and sewing. They also provided refreshments and transportation if needed. Because attendance was poor the women became discouraged. Since then I have come to feel that even though only a few respond we should not discontinue this type of outreach. In fact, it is possible to make a more personal impact in small groups.

Because Head Start has been somewhat downgraded, many will question the validity of such a program as Heart's Nudge with preschool children. However, I know that good was done. I later taught some of the children in kindergarten that I had had in Heart's Nudge and as a teacher I could see the areas in which they had improved. Furthermore, parents were touched by this concern for their children. Not once was I treated disrespectfully by them. I was always invited in no matter how humble a dwelling. I heard many times from the children, "Teacher, you came to my house." Use of the school building enabled us to extend help to more people, and the Future Teachers of America organization supplied needed assistants.

Understanding among the children was enriched, I'm sure. This is best illustrated by two examples. One day a little white girl and a black girl were sitting at the same table working puzzles. After a while the white girl asked her friend, "What color is your skin?" The little colored girl looked down at her arm as if she had never thought about it. She rubbed it and said, "Black." The white girl rubbed it too and said, "That's nice." Then both went on with their puzzles. Another time a black boy was seated at a table and a white boy was using the large building blocks nearby. As the stack got taller, he kept looking over at the black boy and finally stopped long enough to ask, "May I feel your hair?" The black boy went right on with what he was doing and very unconcernedly said, "Sure." The white boy rubbed his hair, smiled, and said, "That's cute." The other smiled back. Prejudice doesn't begin with children, but I honestly believe it can be stopped through them.

During my visits in lower-income homes while I was working with Heart's Nudge, the second project took shape in my mind. The rooms in these homes were so hot, dirty, and crowded that I began to think what a pity it was that someone didn't come and teach the children about Christ so that they could live above their dismal surroundings in the hope that He brings. This idea stayed in my mind and prayers, and from it came the plan that I named "Neighborhoods for Christ" through which I hoped to reach the dirty, unwanted children with the love of Christ right in their own neighborhoods.

This was a very rewarding project because it involved most of our small congregation in one way or another. Basically it was an outdoor vacation church school on a vacant lot in the inner city. The program included Bible study, handcraft, music, worship, games, and refreshments. Of the fifty-seven homes contacted, twenty-six had no children in the elementary level, at seventeen no one was home, two were not interested . . . and twenty-five children were enrolled. Our average daily attendance was seventeen.

We were sure the children enjoyed it because after a severe rainstorm one night I decided the lot would be so wet no one would show up. My daughter and her husband, Cherry and Steve Koehler, went anyway. Much to their surprise most of the children were already there waiting. Since the ground was too wet to walk on we had a short session in the alley.

Lay ministers in our congregation accepted our recommendation and visited in ten of the twelve homes represented. Of these, three were friendly but indifferent, seven were enthusiastic and favored future sessions, and one was interested in learning more about the church. In addition we were successful in placing a speechless five-year-old where he could be tested by a psychologist. These results may not seem spectacular, but who knows what seeds may have been planted in the minds of the children who attended these sessions?

As both parents in more and more families are employed outside the home, there is an increasing need for day care centers for preschool children. Simple baby-sitting is helpful, but many people feel that something more can be made of this service.

[21] Early in January of 1969 another young woman in the Edgewood congregation called me to talk about developing a preschool. I wasn't too responsive. It was a great idea . . . if she did it.

Then I read a series of articles from the book *Education and Ecstasy* by George B. Leonard. I was fascinated with the idea of learning being a joyful experience that children would actively seek to be part of. Maybe a preschool would be a good thing.

With these thoughts in mind I went to a church family camp in July. It was a terrific experience to attend classes on ways to create a serving church that would reflect its concern for humanity through programs that served the needs of people in its area.

Our new church, which was built around an open courtyard, seemed an ideal spot for a day care center. Instead of a preschool where children came for only two hours a day, we really needed a place where children could be cared for all day when circumstances made it impossible for them to be at home. This would not be just a baby-sitting facility but an environment for learning. Every attempt would be made to provide a warm, homelike setting and minimize the institutional atmosphere some day care services have.

When I returned to my congregation I learned there was a special class being created for those who wanted to participate in community development projects. The first project the class chose was the day care center. This would include children who needed preschool by allowing them to attend one or two days a week, yet it would be open from six a.m. to six p.m. five days a week for families who needed care for their children while they worked.

The following weeks were filled with discussion, research, objective planning, solving structural problems, and developing advertising materials. Finally in June 1970 the Edgewood Day Care Center was officially opened. Women in the congregation volunteered to take turns cooking and helping teach. We had two full-time workers who agreed to work for ten dollars a week until September.

Somehow we had expected that people would line up at the door, eager to use our facilities, but this did not happen. It took time for our center to build up a reputation. During the fall months the enrollment increased and salaried help began to replace volunteers. Everything seemed to be going well until midwinter. Then, due to the economy, sickness, and people moving, our enrollment dropped, and we were faced with a severe financial crisis. The volunteers were again called in to help as teacher aides and cooks. I found myself working more and more hours and getting more and more discouraged. Perhaps the Lord wasn't as interested in day care centers as I thought. Perhaps I had just imagined that the Spirit had been leading me. I began to carry a constant prayer in my heart: "Lord, please help me to know if this is a worthwhile work to be doing for You."

In March we had a late snowstorm. My husband took me to work because the streets were so bad. We shoveled the sidewalk and parking lot, but few children were able to get to the center that day. The teacher couldn't get there either, so I called the cook and told her to stay home—I would fix lunch for the six children who had come. By two o'clock that afternoon these children had already been picked up because the entire city was at a standstill. As I straightened up the craft area, I was suddenly aware of the warmth of the Spirit penetrating my mind and flowing through me, giving me strength and joy.

Once more I was assured of the validity of the dream that I had claimed as my own but which had become the dream of a number of families. This day care center was the result of a congregation desiring to implement God's will now. This common desire had brought us to the frontier of our faith where faith becomes action—not just passive acceptance.

* * *

In the not too distant past large families were the norm because parents needed the labor of their children: girls to help the mother make clothing, prepare the food, and keep the house; boys to help the father produce the living. This type of society no longer exists, but there is still the necessity for young people to feel necessary. Teen-agers need the satisfaction of working at useful jobs and earning money. It isn't always easy for them to find such jobs.

Several years ago four young couples started an employment service for youth looking for jobs to help finance their education. Each member of a committee contacted the sources available to him through the personnel department of his own company, giving the director a copy of the application which might be submitted to him by a young person and giving assurance that each applicant would be carefully screened so that the committee could vouch for him and the kind of work that he could do.

The first year eleven young people were placed. The following year every personnel department asked for more summer workers. At last count over seventy-eight young people of high school and college age had found employment because a few people cared.

* * *

Young people of every country and culture frequently need educational help to fit them for better jobs. Better jobs mean a better contribution to society and a better standard of living for themselves and their families. Many governments do not finance secondary and technical schools. In these countries poorer nationals look to more affluent people for financial aid. In receiving such aid it is tremendously important that they be made to feel that they are helping themselves rather than being recipients of charity.

[22] As the need for some means of helping young church members in Mexico to continue their education became especially apparent in the spring of 1962, ideas began to take shape. On returning to Saltillo, Mexico, from our world church conference in April, Bob and I found that two young

men in the congregation, through no fault of their own, had lost their jobs during our absence. Since both depended on their earnings to stay in school, they had dropped out. We couldn't see their losing the whole year's credits, so we advanced the funds to help them finish out the year. With interest developing in the possibility of two Honduran girls coming to Saltillo to further their education, we began to think of the best way to assist these young people.

We decided on a Student Center—a dormitory setup, where the youth would live in a Christian study-adapted atmosphere and from which they would go out to secondary and professional schools in town. (Saltillo is an excellent place to further one's education, as it has more schools per capita than any other city in Mexico.) For our Student Center we needed an appropriate house, a dorm mother, financing for the rent, food, and students' school expenses. We wrote about the matter to church officials who "smiled upon the venture" and also to a wealthy member in Independence, with whom we'd talked about opportunities in Latin America. This good man paid the rent for three years on a large house. We arranged for one of the women of our congregation, Rosario Lopez, to be the dorm mother and in charge of meals. Happily this also fulfilled a financial need for her and her family. The cost of food, utilities, school registrations, and books was estimated and averaged per student so that interested persons could sponsor a student. We found that many people were glad to help these youths further their education in this way. Others who could not help on a regular basis made contributions which helped us get bunk beds, tables, and other essential items.

We called the center "Centro Estudiantil Restaumex." The first year we had seven students, the next fourteen, the next twenty-four. By the third year, we felt the need for more space, more work for the students to do so they would feel they were contributing in part to their own support, and some way for them to provide for their own needs. After looking at a number of large houses, my father, Carroll L. Olson, and Bob invested in a fourteen-acre property with a large house, several smaller buildings, many pecan trees, and agricultural land. It was only a fifteen-minute walk from many of the schools and on a bus line to others.

Whereas at first the only jobs the students had to do were to help with the cleaning and dishes, now there were gardens to tend, lawns to mow and water, continual repairs and improvements. Also there was plenty of space for recreation—ball, swimming, and even horseback riding.

Of the sixty-seven young people who have been or are still at the Student Center, four have been graduated from commercial academies, six as teachers, six as technicians, four as engineers, two as nurses, two as "licenciados" in economy and psychology. Fifteen others have been graduated from secondary school and are either still studying or working at jobs. Three national ministers met their wives at the Center. Twenty young people were baptized after finding the church through the Center (in some cases this has extended to family members at home).

Although both my husband and my father have died, their vision of people better equipped to support and educate their families and contribute to society, as well as better prepared to serve the church, continues. Rosario Lopez, now a widow also, continues to help me. With Efrain Zuniga—Student Center chaplain, Saltillo pastor, and graduate in psychology—we make a pretty good team.

Persons or groups who sponsor students receive receipts from a United States benevolent foundation, but more than an income tax deduction they receive the satisfaction of knowing that they're participants in this team of workers that help Latin American youths reach out to broader horizons of learning and service than would be possible otherwise.

* * *

In society's praiseworthy desire to rehabilitate its drunks, the children in alcoholic homes may be forgotten. Their problems, resentments, and hostilities too often are swept under the rug. Alateens, a natural outgrowth of Alcoholics Anonymous, gives concerned adults a chance to help teenagers weather the emotional storms of family life with alcoholic parents. An editor, author, poet (whose name must be withheld because of A.A. tradition) has worked for years with this organization. Her story is a dramatic one.

"I *hate* my mother and father!" All eyes turned to Jo Ellen but no one said anything. The hurt, angry words tumbled out—the too-often-heard tale of a child caught in the cross-currents of the family disease, alcoholism. "As soon as school is out I'm going to run away."

My mind slipped back to an Arizona morning when I fought my own battle with "running away." Signs of the midnight skirmish—tracings of meat pie across the kitchen floor and down a newly finished door where my husband had thrown it in a drunken tantrum—filled me with despair. I turned from the mess and gazed out the window toward the mountains: "I will lift up mine eyes unto the hills, from whence cometh my help." But this morning no help came. How easy it would be to drive the Ford up the twisting road to the nearest summit and send it plummeting to the rocks below. If I could just be sure it would kill us all, the three children and me . . . such an easy solution to insufferable problems. . . . I toyed with the idea all that day.

Despair can be the "sickness unto death" and I had

known little else for three years. The unrealistic aura of hope my husband's six sober months had fashioned with the help of Alcoholics Anonymous had long since disappeared. My prayers bounced off the ceiling. My alienation from God, friends, and family—my floundering and subsequent self-loathing—activated the instinct for self-destruction.

I'm thankful for that still small voice that turned me back toward life again. Two years later my husband was celebrating a "first birthday" in A.A. and I was rebuilding my own shattered self with the help of understanding A.A. families and loyal church friends.

Those were the days of the A.A. auxiliary and the spouses of alcoholics developed their own forms of group therapy using A.A.'s Twelve Steps as a guide. When the Al-Anon Family Group surfaced, with national headquarters and printed helps, the A.A. auxiliary to which I belonged promptly "signed up." Alateens, for teen-age children of alcoholics, were a logical outgrowth of the Al-Anon Family Group.

I have known many Jo Ellens in my years of helping to sponsor Alateen groups. The children of alcoholics are among the "battered" children of our society. Their scars are not always visible, but the terrible insecurity, the futility, the actual deprivation of physical as well as emotional needs make for shattering distortions of self-image. Most children assume a seldom articulated sense of guilt for the family situation. They often become "loners" and rarely relate to their peer group.

Alateen groups, now international in scope, have worked miracles for many of these children. Teen-agers are helped to see that they are not responsible for the alcoholism in their homes and that they need not be controlled by it. A New York City Alateen group states it this way:

"In Alateen we have learned to become individuals. We try to realize that alcoholism is a disease. In studying the Twelve Steps of Alcoholics Anonymous, we learn to accept the fact that we are powerless over alcohol and that we *can* develop the ability to detach ourselves emotionally from our parents' problem, while continuing to love them."

Surprisingly enough, membership in Alateens is not always encouraged by Al-Anon and A.A. members. Parents often fear that the meetings are gossip or "gripe" sessions where the children pry open family closets and place the skeletons on public display. This is far from the truth. Weekly Alateen meetings are usually planned. Guest speakers at our meetings have included doctors, judges, a police chief, a psychologist, a school counselor, a Catholic priest, several ministers, a physical education teacher, and several youth leaders. At least one meeting a month is devoted to study of A.A.'s Twelve Steps as we have adapted them for our group:

1. Admitted I was powerless over alcoholism in my home.
2. Came to believe that a Power greater than myself could restore me to normal living.
3. Made a decision to turn my life over to God as I understand him.
4. Made a searching and fearless moral inventory of myself.
5. Admitted to God, to myself, and to someone else the exact nature of my wrongs.
6. Was entirely ready for God to remove my defects of character.
7. Humbly asked Him to remove my shortcomings.
8. Made a list of people I had wronged and became willing to make amends to them all.
9. Made amends to such people where possible except when it would injure them or others.
10. Continue to take personal inventory and when wrong promptly admit it.
11. Seek through prayer and meditation to improve my contact with God, praying only for knowledge of his will concerning me and the courage to carry that out.

12. Having had a spiritual awakening as a result of these steps, I will carry this message to others and practice these principles in all my affairs.

Alateens plan and lead these discussions. They also act as guest speakers for neighboring Alateen groups. Occasionally a meeting is built around a question such as "Is your unhappiness at home affecting your schoolwork?" "Do you feel inferior, frustrated, depressed?" "Can learning about other people's problems help you to understand your own?" "Do you give enough time and thought to Alateens to replace resentment and self-pity?" Once a group has developed comradery and sense of purpose it is largely self-sufficient and the wise sponsor moves quietly into the background.

Many years have passed since that day my Arizona mountains denied their strength. As I have worked at mending my own life I have been given the tools to help others do the same. That's the whole A.A. story. But I have known sorrow as well as joy—sorrow when I have heard that one of *my* teens has been arrested for drunk driving or possession of marijuana. Sorrow when a teen who is so obviously lost attends one meeting and writes it off as bunk. But oh the joy when a former Alateen, now grown and married, joins me as sponsor of a new Alateen group. Joy, when a gray-haired gentleman says, "Remember me? You talked to my A.A. group about Alateens ten years ago and I've been an Alateen sponsor—and sober—ever since."

And the greatest joy of all is hearing Jo Ellen say, in an open A.A. meeting, "I once thought I hated my parents. I planned to run away. But my friends in Alateens helped me to see that I only hated the disease of alcoholism. They showed me how, by changing my attitudes, I could make things getter at home. And they helped me to believe once more in a Higher Power. For that I am thankful."

The types of service to young people explored in this chapter are neither unusual nor definitive. They are simply representative of thousands of service projects being implemented in many areas. People with vision and imagination can see needs and solutions to those needs—possibly no further away than their own backyards.

CHAPTER FIVE

Service to Senior Citizens

[23] At the start of the year the Toronto-Metropolitan District had a unique opportunity to sponsor a government financed project devoted to meeting the needs of pensioners in the area of the downtown congregation.

Uppermost was the idea of helping these people to remain independent in their own quarters, thus preventing the need for them to enter nursing homes. I decided to become actively involved in the project, so I quit my clerical work and pitched in.

In the back of my mind was the desire to fulfill what I think is an important work of the church—that of serving in the community. After a fine experience with the Older Youth Service Corps I was determined to commit a portion of my life to serving on a full-time, no-charge basis. The sponsoring of this project by the church meant that I had an opportunity to deal with people of an age group with which I had had little contact before.

This community project consisted of a staff of eight people. Four were members of my church; the rest belonged to other denominations. The backgrounds of these people were truly interesting. Although the director had an MSW degree, the staff members were not in professional social work.

My initial experience with a retired person was memorable. I was assigned to drive a Ukrainian-speaking man home from the hospital, where he had had serious abdominal surgery. After that I was to visit him often to see that he had enough food and was physically able to care for himself.

The man was reluctant to leave the hospital where he had received lots of care. At home, he knew, he would be all alone. After much persuasion a social worker in the hospital convinced him that he would be all right. In broken English he tried to tell me how wonderful the woman in the hospital had been to him—they had talked often in his native tongue. Then he told me how frightened he was of going home. He would be alone because all of his family were still living in a communist country. No one would be around to see if he was all right. There would be no one to talk to. By visiting him for several weeks I was able to reassure him that he wasn't alone, and that I wanted to help him.

As we chatted about our lives, I received the impression that this lonely man had a deep faith in God. I found this impression reinforced not only by listening to him but by seeing the evidences of his belief—a picture of Christ over the kitchen sink and numerous Bibles in different languages in his room. During our chats I discovered he was a member of the Ukrainian Orthodox Church. Together we shared our belief in Christ. And because he thought that I resembled his son who lived overseas our relationship continued to grow. We felt truly like brothers in Christ.

This experience has enhanced my love and appreciation for those who have lived most of their lives. Many in their twilight years are devoted people who can strengthen younger persons with more energy. We need to be more considerate of these people who often feel neglected and unneeded. They still have much to offer. I have been truly blessed by this and other experiences with senior citizens.

It is rather unusual and certainly refreshing to hear of a young man doing this type of volunteer work. It is not so unusual but still refreshing to hear of the many women who consider this an important part of their stewardship.

* * *

[24] Perhaps the reason I spend so much time visiting those who are sick and shut-in is because I know how they feel—I've been in that situation myself. Many years ago I was in a car accident in which my sister died. My experience in the hospital at that time had made me sensitive to the needs of others who are confined to sick rooms. Some time later I suffered a fall while standing on a ladder picking cherries. The doctor who set the many broken bones told me, "Think of the many things you will still be able to do. You have good eyes and good ears, so you can still see and hear. You can still talk. but the one thing you will never be able to do again is walk. So many bones were broken that you will no longer have a balanced body."

This seemed the final sentencing to the life of a cripple . . . but God had other plans for me. One day while I was alone in my house, I heard a voice saying, "Get up out of your chair and walk around the walker." I was healed! As I grew stronger I returned to normal activity. Since that time I have felt a great deal of empathy for those, particularly older people, who cannot move about by themselves.

Now I call on the residents at Resthaven, Binger Home, Windsor Estates, and the Jackson County Old Folks Home. I also visit patients in local hospitals and those who are confined to their homes. Some have no one else to visit them and feel so alone. I often try to take another person with me—two visitors are better than one and the other person just may become interested in making such visits a regular habit, too.

I find there are many little services I can perform for elderly people in my neighborhood. I often provide transportation for them when they need to go to the grocery store, to church, to visit friends or relatives, or just for a pleasure drive around the countryside.

Every Wednesday the Sunshine Club provides a program, and I help with the entertainment after the government-sponsored dinner for the senior citizens.

Often the Good Spirit tells me where I should go and what I should do on a particular day. In obedience to this "impulse" I have visited sick and elderly friends who have died shortly afterwards. How sad I would have felt if I had not had this last visit with them! I thank God for his urging me to call on someone who may need loving comfort from a friend.

Rest homes, convalescent homes, and retirement villages are springing up in most countries of the Western world. Some of these are private establishments for affluent senior citizens who can afford to pay handsomely for care and comfort. Some are financed by churches for their retired ministers and missionaries. Some are funded by the government. Many, even though partially financed by federal or church money, still depend on fairly high rent from their patrons. Australians have come up with an interesting contrast.

[6] One of the significant areas of outreach in Australia is the program for Senior Citizen Housing. These units are now

located in five metropolitan centers: Brisbane, Newcastle, Sydney, Melbourne, and Adelaide. They are designed so that elderly people can care for themselves; there is no outside maintenance, and furnishings are arranged for easy house-keeping. For safety, grip handles are placed in showers; milk bottles and trash can be set out without the residents having to go outside. Most units consist of a bedroom, lounge-dining area, kitchen, and bathroom. Basic rental charges run $3.50 a week for a single person and $4.50 for a married couple. Those who are able to do so are expected to make a cash donation when they become residents. These homes are financed jointly by the Commonwealth Department of Social Services and the church.

In many cities church groups or women's clubs operate a service called "Meals on Wheels" which transports meals to homebound people who are not able to prepare hot, nourishing food for themselves.

* * *

The "Loaves and Fishes" program in Portland, Oregon, is an example of interdenominational cooperation to meet the nutritional needs of senior citizens. These church women serve balanced meals three times a week in areas of high concentration of the elderly. Volunteers deliver meals to a few who cannot leave their homes due to physical handicaps. Many older people are not financially or physically able to prepare the food they must have for good health; others lack the interest to do so because they live alone. It is for them that "Loaves and Fishes" was created. In addition to meals served at the center, the women sponsor games, group singing, and other social activities before and after the meal to help fill the void in so many lonely lives. Special events such as picnics, boat trips, and bus tours are part of the program. The center also serves as a referral agent to inform participants of services available to them through government and volunteer agencies.

* * *

The women's department of an Indianapolis church has made service to its senior citizens a continuing project. Once a month the women provide a potluck dinner after the Sunday morning worship. Only senior citizens are invited. The chairman of the service committee says that a wonderful spirit is present at these dinners, and the women feel it a privilege when it is their turn to serve.

The group also maintains an individualized tribute to each of these elderly people. Each year the single senior citizen receives a cake or fruit basket on his birthday; married couples receive theirs on their wedding anniversary. This service is performed by individual women on a rotating basis. A member of the Service Committee keeps a record of all the birthdays and anniversaries and is responsible for calling each woman when it is her turn. She then prepares the cake or fruit basket and delivers it personally.

The chairman of the Service Committee reports that these little kindnesses have changed the whole atmosphere of the congregation. "It's as though love has been let loose," she says.

* * *

The Skylark Band (a church sponsored girls' organization) in Kitchener, Ontario, as one of its projects plans special activities for the women at the Senior Citizens' Home in Bridgeport. The girls celebrate birthdays, provide programs for special occasions, play games, and just plain visit their "foster grandmothers." For them, bridging a two-generation gap is not just being nice . . . it's having fun. And for the "grandmothers" it's better than medicine the doctor prescribes.

* * *

Several members of the Fairland Home Demonstration Club in Oklahoma regularly visit the local Rest Home one afternoon a week. Elderly people who are ambulatory walk down to the reception room; others are pushed there in wheelchairs. All come to hear the women sing the "old hymns," and often they too join in the singing. Those who are bedridden don't miss out on all the fun; they hear through their open bedroom doors. And the visiting women go through the building chatting with all the residents and nurses before they leave. No one ever feels left out.

* * *

A group of women have organized a unique service project simply by contacting several funeral homes in the area and offering to pick up any unclaimed flowers. Many times expensive floral arrangements are thrown in the trash. When a funeral director calls the chairman, she in turn contacts a worker who picks up the flowers, takes them home, and rearranges them in vases and small containers for hospitals, shut-ins, and rest homes. A special visit is made for the presentation. A card bearing the name of the church is enclosed, and on the back is a handwritten message of hope and cheer. This brings joy to both the giver and receiver.

* * *

Westminster Village is a church-operated retirement home where residents live in apartments appropriate to their needs and have access to medical and custodial care.

The women of a nearby church decided, as part of their stewardship, to visit the residents on a one-to-one basis. The medical staff of the village was just starting occupational therapy and considered this offer to be the answer to their prayers for help. The women could function not only as visitors but act as aides in helping the elderly residents with handcraft, games, and exercise.

Since then the women of this church have been going to Westminster Village on a rotating basis. On Tuesdays they can help with crafts, on Wednesdays with games or walks, and on Thursdays with ceramics. On other days they just visit with the patients.

Lillian Porter has taken on a unique service project. She is a one-woman shopping service for the residents who cannot or don't want to leave the grounds. She shops for them every week, even exchanging items which aren't satisfactory for one reason or another.

It would be hard to say who benefits more from this project—the residents who look forward to these visitors or the women who have learned to love being with their elderly friends.

* * *

The Towers is a low-income housing development for older people. Several churches of the community participate in sponsoring Sunday worship services for the residents. Ministers and laymen go out every Sunday afternoon to conduct church services in a large meeting room.

* * *

A group of women who like to sing together have adopted the project of going to senior citizen homes, nursing and convalescent homes, orphanages, and rehabilitation centers to sing for the patients. As in so many service projects, these women feel that they receive more than they give.

During a recent Christmas season the group went caroling at the Turtle Creek Convalescent Home. Like pied pipers, they gathered a following of the ambulatory patients on each floor who trailed after them to the floor above. As they sang in the sun room of one ward, they noticed an old lady sitting in a straight chair, staring vacantly into space. As they sang carol after carol, she slowly turned to face them. Then responding further she began to rock back and forth in her nonrocking chair. Finally her lips began to move as she joined in singing "Silent Night" along with them. Suddenly an aide broke away from the group standing by a door, went across the room, and knelt beside the old lady.

"You don't know what you've done for her," another aide told the singers in a low voice. "She's been here for weeks, and this is the first time she has given us any sign that she could even speak."

It must have been a very special Christmas for those women who shared with God in this little miracle of love.

Bertha Heater—a pretty, petite Independence housewife—"retired" from her job at the local library in order to devote more time to helping the patients in Cottage 1 at the state hospital in Marshall, Missouri. She and her husband Clarence have been making the seventy-mile drive there nearly every weekend since their son Donald was admitted twenty years ago. An illness which crippled him and stopped his mental development at age six made life in the mainstream of society more and more frustrating for him as he grew to maturity. At the hospital he has found his place; he can care for himself, help others whose disabilities are greater than his own, and assist with the laundry. In fact, when his parents take him to Independence for the holidays he is eager to return to the hospital. For him, it is home.

The Heaters have done much to make Cottage 1 a pleasant place not only for their son but for the other 250 patients. Enlisting the help of four other couples who had children in the hospital, they began by redecorating the place in cheerful pastels instead of institutional gray. Adding pictures and drapes they were able to give the minimally furnished rooms a less stark appearance. Eventually they provided a stereo record player and several TV sets. They also extended the opportunity to help to church and social clubs in the greater Kansas City area, and now no Christmas goes by without each patient receiving gifts. And there are programs and parties presented by church youth groups. Thanksgiving, Valentine's Day, Easter, and the Fourth of July are all occasions for celebrating.

Early in her experience with the patients Bertha realized that they needed more than pleasant surroundings to brighten their lives. They needed to belong to somebody (most of them seldom see relatives; some never do). It happened one day when her own son had been following her around calling her "Mama." A little black boy came up to her and asked, "Are you my mama too?" She put her arms around him and said, "Of course." Then all the other neglected boys wanted her for their mother also.

Interestingly, at least half of her "boys" are older than she is. One of them, a wizened sexigenarian named Joey, is particularly close to her because of an experience they shared nearly a decade ago. One Sunday when she arrived at the hospital she heard that Joey was in the infirmary, so she went immediately to see him. "He was running a high fever and looked so pathetic I wondered how I could possibly help him . . . but I decided to try. I took his hand and said, 'Joey, it's daytime now, but when it's night and the stars are shining, I'll be home. There I'll kneel beside my bed and ask God to make you better. When you look out and see the stars, remember that I'll be praying for you.' He looked up and asked, 'Mama, how well do you know God?' 'I know him, Joey,' I answered, 'but after tonight I think I'll know him even better.' The next week I found Joey completely recovered. He could hardly wait to tell me about it. 'God did make me better, and now I know him too.' ''

People never grow too old to need love. Bertha Heater has found a very special way to meet that need for some of society's most unloved, unlovely "children."

CHAPTER SIX

Going the Second Mile

[25] A young woman sits in the lawyer's office. Her husband is irresponsible. He spends what he wants, does what he wants, and leaves her to support the family as well as keep house and care for the children. Three weeks ago she told him to leave. He did. There have been fights and separations before. The problem has gone on for many years. Now the woman says she wants a divorce.

The lawyer tells the woman that from the facts she has related it appears she is entitled to a divorce. If she goes through with the divorce she will probably get a judgment for a substantial amount of child support based upon her husband's present income level. But, statistically, a substantial amount of child support owed never gets paid.

"When did you and your husband last have intercourse?" The lawyer asks a seemingly unlawyer-like question.

"Last night," the woman admits, looking a bit surprised and sheepish. "Tom came over for a while."

The lawyer recommends a marriage counselor and advises the woman to see him whether or not she decides to go through with the divorce. After years of vacillation, she will find the decision to go through with the divorce difficult. The lawyer offers no opinion on whether she should get the divorce but urges her to make a careful, responsible decision. He repeats the importance of seeing a counselor.

"But I told you, I have already made my decision," the woman interjects. "I want a divorce now. That's final and irrevocable."

"It's customary for lawyers to get their fees in advance in divorce cases," the lawyer explains. "The standard fee for an uncontested divorce is $350 plus a $45 filing fee. I'll file as soon as you can raise $395. But I would appreciate it if you would discuss your decision with the marriage counselor. I'm not convinced that deep down you have really made that decision yet. You've had separations before. This time I want to see you get to the bottom of the problem and solve it."

The woman does see the marriage counselor. Two months later she writes the lawyer a letter. Its tone is that of a communication with a friend. "Tom and I have been back together for six weeks," she writes. "But it isn't working out. I've got the $395 now, and have decided to go through with the divorce. I'll be in in about two weeks. I'm so glad you persuaded me to go to that marriage counselor. He's been so helpful. Thank you for being concerned that I do this thing right."

The woman never comes in. The lawyer does not make the divorce fee.

Months later the lawyer runs into the marriage counselor at a luncheon and asks about his client. "She came for a while, but then she stopped coming," the counselor replies. "I wonder if she ever solved her problem."

* * *

The boy has been a problem since childhood. At eight or nine he wet his bed regularly. At ten he was caught stealing several times. By fifteen he was experimenting with drugs. At seventeen he was told to leave home by his father, a man of harsh discipline and condemning judgments. He began to wander about and soon wandered into more trouble. Now, at nineteen he stands convicted of a drug charge for the second time and is on the verge of being sent to prison. Probation has failed. The boy has also been jailed several times on theft charges and has apparently not learned from the experience. Just that day the boy's bond was revoked because he was caught using more drugs. His arms display numerous fresh needle marks. Now he, the lawyer, and two policemen are en route to a hospital in a police car. The boy has taken an overdose of drugs and is unconscious in the front seat, muttering incoherently. His hands are manacled behind his back.

The lawyer persuades the policemen not to lodge additional charges against the boy for the drugs found on him when he was arrested. He also sees to it that his client will be shackled to his bed with a leg iron when he resumes consciousness and that the nurses are warned to lock the medicine cabinets. He does not want his client creating more problems before he is sentenced.

The boy has been in trouble on this drug charge for five months, but neither of his parents has visited him. He has had several arguments with his father on the telephone though. The father seemingly has abandoned all responsibility for the boy but reserves the right to chew him out for his misdeeds and to let him know how much of a disappointment he is to his family. The lawyer calls the father and reports on the situation. So far the father has not offered to pay the lawyer for representing his son. But the lawyer knows he will be angry if he is not called and told of this new development.

The lawyer courteously explains the situation to the father. The father is angry at the boy but does not want to see him go to prison. In one breath he speaks of having the boy "get what's coming to him." In the next, he expresses concern for his son. He listens when the lawyer says the young man is sick and prison will only make his problem worse. Finally, the lawyer lays it on the line to the father. "I want you to come out here and see this boy and give him some love," he says. "And I want you to stop disparaging him." The lawyer's tone is firm but uncondemning.

The father is angry at what the lawyer has said, but he listens. Underneath his anger is a stronger emotion—love. Finally, the father promises to think it over. "Think this over, too," the lawyer follows up. "No matter what you do, you cannot change your son's behavior. You can only change your own behavior to an attitude of love, and hope he'll respond in kind. But don't sell short the possibility that this will produce a positive response. I've seen it happen many times."

That night the lawyer visits the boy and tells him he cannot change his father's behavior but if he will change his own attitude, he might see some corresponding changes in his father's.

Ultimately, the father visits the boy and, for the time being at least, the attitudes of both seem to be changed. The boy is again sentenced to probation on condition that he voluntarily commit himself to a private mental hospital near his family's residence and engage in regular joint counseling sessions with the family. A prison sentence is imposed but suspended to provide motivation for the boy to follow through with the program. The father agrees to allow his insurance to pay the hospital bills.

Boy and father go off. The lawyer is confident the program is the best available but wonders if it will work.

* * *

The woman lists her debts for the lawyer. She owes thousands to finance companies and department stores. She is unemployed. "I can't work. I'm on tranquilizers," she says. "My nerves are bad."

Next she lists her assets. She has a new stereo set, a color TV, appliances, furniture—all secured for loans. She has been paying on some items for years. Others have been bought only recently. For each item she is paying between 10 and 30 percent of the purchase price extra in finance charges.

The lawyer asks about the woman's employment history. She has had many employers. The woman explains elaborately how she lost her last job. She performed well, and the boss gave her compliments. She was even going to get a raise and a promotion, he liked her work so well. All her bosses have liked her work. She gets lots of compliments. But then her boss fired her suddenly without explanation, just as the others did. She doesn't know exactly why he fired her but thinks it has something to do with the fact that her "nerves" got the better of her and she began to do some things more slowly than usual.

The lawyer explains the law about bankruptcy and gives his opinion that it would be good if the woman could make a new start. However, the problem would not really be solved unless the woman could learn to operate on a cash, as opposed to a credit, basis. For several hours the lawyer and the woman make the elaborate listings of debts, creditors, assets, etc., involved in a bankruptcy proceeding.

Finally, after all the data has been collected, the woman volunteers one other bit of information. "I'm trying to make a big decision," she says. "A man wants to marry me. I have to decide by next week whether to do it or not. Will this affect my bankruptcy case?"

"Have you told the man about your debts?" the lawyer asks.

"Well . . . not exactly."

The lawyer arranges a discussion of the marriage decision with the social worker who had referred the woman for bankruptcy advice. The marriage issue is new to the social worker, though he has been counseling the woman regularly for months. Eventually the bankruptcy goes through, but the marriage does not occur during the proceedings. The lawyer is skeptical that the woman will resist the temptation to buy on credit in the future, but at least she now has a chance to live without the financial worries she has been experiencing.

* * *

A man sitting before the lawyer's desk suddenly starts gasping and coughing. The lawyer offers a glass of water but the man's convulsing is too violent for him to accept it. Five minutes later the coughing spell is still going on, and the lawyer considers calling for an ambulance. Then the spell stops, and the man takes the water. "It's cirrhosis of the liver," the man explains cryptically. "I used to be an alcoholic, but I gave it up two months ago." The man has the red eye rims of a long-term alcoholic. The smell of the whiskey he drank just before entering the office permeates the air. The man's speech and demeanor display some signs of alcoholic brain damage.

"You want me to apply for a hardship driver's license for you now that your license has been revoked," the lawyer says. The man's traffic offense record indicates the revocation occurred because he was convicted of driving while under the influence of alcohol. The arrest was at the scene of an accident which occurred while he was driving to work.

"I'm afraid that before I can convince a judge to give you a special privilege to drive to and from work I'm going to need some proof that you won't be drinking anymore," the lawyer tells his client.

"Don't worry, I've stopped for good now," the client replies.

The lawyer tells the client his promise not to drink will not be good enough for the judge.

A modification of the man's probation is arranged so that he will be required to take antibuse—a drug that discourages alcohol consumption while it remains in the patient's system—for two years. Weekly alcoholism counseling is a part of the program. A drying-out period in a hospital is also provided for. The lawyer carefully gets his client to sign a statement that he wants all this. He signs because he wants to drive.

Ultimately, the client is dried out, put on antibuse, and given limited privileges to drive to and from work. If he continues to take the drug, the deterioration of his brain and liver will be arrested. He will no longer vomit when he awakens each morning. To him, these are mere side effects of his application to drive again. He had not thought them worth giving up the bottle. But if he stays with the program, they will mean more to him and to his family as his life goes on.

* * *

A Christian lawyer must be satisfied to work for temporary successes. There are no long-term certainties for most people in deep trouble except that unless the pattern changes misery will go on. The lawyer comes into a client's life only at a brief moment, and then the life goes on out of the lawyer's influence again. Yet the moment in which the lawyer's services are rendered can be a turning point. This is so because many people come to lawyers at times of crisis when they are desperate enough to consider repentance. The lawyer who is aware of that opportunity can render a great Christian service.

It is a service hard to perform because so often the lawyer must act before there is time to get to know the client well. Moreover, the lawyer is in business to make money and has high overhead costs. If he is any kind of businessman, he soon finds a conflict between his business judgment and the demands of those clients who offer the greatest opportunities for Christian ministry. Not only have such people often messed up their lives to the point where they cannot pay a lawyer but they also require that he devote time to their personal needs for counsel and concern apart from the time required to serve their legal interests. That time is, from a business standpoint, inefficient. The lawyer must daily decide whether God or Mammon will be his master. It is often a hard choice to make because it is not always immediately clear what is in God's interest and what solely interests Mammon.

Finally, the lawyer's business is built upon pleasing his clients, yet people in trouble are often selfish and unrealistic in their thinking. They need to be told things they do not want to hear. It is relatively easy for a lawyer to say, with professional authority, "You have a bad case" or "The law will not allow you to do that." It is harder to say, "It's none of my business, but you are making a mess of your life, and it's going to go on unless you change something." Yet the lawyer who cares about his clients must often do the latter as well as the former, risking their displeasure with him.

It is difficult, but rewarding, to try to be a Christian lawyer. But then, it is difficult, but rewarding, to be any kind of Christian.

To a large extent this book is based on the supposition that people who truly want to serve have naturally chosen a useful trade, industry, or profession that contributes to life instead of merely taking from it. Some professions are service-oriented—doctors, nurses, dentists, ministers, and teachers, for example. However, these are not the only useful vocations by any means; also needed are mechanics, plumbers, electricians, carpenters, bricklayers, chemists, pharmacists, stenographers, typists, store clerks, editors, accountants, cooks, waiters, waitresses, bus boys, factory workers, truck drivers, housewives . . . the list is endless. The only qualification is that the person give an honest day's labor for a day's pay in a job that is useful in the Christian society. That last statement is qualified, because some jobs which seem useful to non-Christians may not be necessary or even desirable in the Christian life-style.

Our Christian faith should be so much a part of us—so inextricably mingled with our every action and thought—that it will influence the way we perform our daily work. A Christian finds that he has no choice: he feels compelled to use his vocation to promote God's work in the lives around him. Just as the Christian lawyer uses every counseling opportunity on the side of the angels, so Christians in any vocation will find themselves led to go the second mile in the performance of their daily work.

Sometimes the special service may grow directly out of the job itself. Let's look at teachers who use their skill—plus God—to help students achieve what would otherwise seem to be impossible.

[26] She was eleven years old and in fourth grade when my husband and I first saw her. She had been failed twice, and on the basis of its testing the school was recommending that she be placed in a class for the mentally retarded. Her parents had asked for an additional evaluation of her learning problems.

She was unable to read or write, except for a few words. Number concepts did not connect to arithmetic symbols. She could add 6 and 3 and get 2, and subtract 4 from 7 and get 9. Although her basic visual acuity was normal, she had visual perceptual problems. She had difficulty in catching a ball, and she was unable to judge the relationship lines in a geometric figure and draw them in proper orientation to each other. She also had auditory perceptual problems. When spoken word patterns changed, as when *pan* was changed to *plan,* she couldn't judge whether a sound had been added, taken away, or substituted. This prevented her from verifying the logic of our reading and spelling system. She kept her head down and answered, "I don't know," to most information questions. The few times she did meet my gaze, however, the aching look in her eyes told me there was something to reach. This was further verified by the fact that although most of her subtest scores on an intelligence test were three years or more below her age level, two scores did fall within the normal range.

I scheduled her for some exploratory teaching, and began the work of finding out what she did know so we could build from there. She was sure she would never be able to learn to read. She had become so convinced that she was dumb she was afraid even to try to think. I sensed that if I were successful in getting her to try, but then unsuccessful in teaching her to read, she probably would never try again. I felt a deep responsibility for the potential of her life, and I prayed before every teaching session that the Lord's creative power would inspire my mind. Her need must not go unmet because of inadequacy on my part.

Using a dialogue and discovery approach, I assured Sherry that any answer she gave could be accepted. We could explore an answer for its points of relevance, and also its points of irrelevance, using it to find our way further. Little by little she found there was no need to panic at a question. She found that answers could involve a process of several thinking steps, and that the trick was to find a relevant point from which to start thinking. Her limited vocabulary was enlarged through enriching sensory experiences. She gradually developed confidence in her ability to verbalize, to use words for thinking and for focusing her perceptions, and to process and connect the information from all of her senses in every problem-solving situation.

I studied volumes as I searched for new ideas on the development of basic skills in reading, spelling, and arithmetic. It helped, but it wasn't enough, so I built each session empirically, using what we had discovered the session before. The Spirit provided insights, and yet there were plateaus and even setbacks. Each time we hit one I would counsel with my husband whose field is linguistics, and he and I would examine our goal with Sherry in terms of our problem of the moment. Again and again he was able, out of his years of extensive reading, to refer me to an exact author and an exact principle which illumined the situation. I began to realize that this was not accidental, but I wondered at the process involved. I knew that I had received inspiration as I had prayed about how to make abstract concepts sufficiently concrete for Sherry to grasp, but I wondered about the directing of my husband's mind. To my knowledge, he was not overtly praying about our work with Sherry. At a later time it was made known to me that this was possible because he possessed such a basic humility—*his very life was a prayer.*

And so it was accomplished. Verbal abilities were developed and linked to thinking and reasoning activities; auditory perceptual competency was established and linked to reading and spelling activities; visual-motor skills were extended. Within two years Sherry had closed enough of her educational gaps to proceed on her own. She is now completing her senior year in high school and leading a full life. She is housekeeper and baby-sitter in a motherless home while carrying the expected schedule of classes. She drives her own car. She is considering entering college. It is doubtful that her life could have moved in these directions had we not had the guidance of the Holy Spirit in working with her.

There have been others whose stories are equally as interesting and encouraging. There was Martha, who was mentally retarded and whose speech was unintelligible. At twelve she was physically attractive, but she was withdrawing more and more from the world around her because of her inability to communicate. She was unable to tolerate any unfamiliar situation unless a member of her family was present, and even at home she had begun to run and hide when guests came. Performance tests indicated a probable mental level of about seven years, and a seven-year-old can certainly operate at a language level in which basic needs and even hopes and plans and dreams can be expressed.

An effort had to be made. It could make the difference between a life which could assume human proportions, and one which remained at an animal level. Again, this was too large a responsibility to be undertaken without prayer.

It was difficult to establish trust and confidence, but with patience it came. Again, with a dialogue and discovery approach, I conveyed to Martha that all her responses could be accepted. For a long time she kept up a smoke screen of short attention or calculated inattention plus bizarre and distracting behavior mannerisms, but these gradually disappeared. As auditory perceptual judgment was established she began to be self-generating and self-corrective in her speech and language patterns. Within a year her speech was completely intelligible and she could communicate with anyone. We then began to work on reading and writing. Under my husband's guidance she showed promise of reaching the level of her oral language skill.

By the time she was a sophomore in the high school's special education program, three- and four-syllable words were beginning to appear in her conversation, and she was able to read and write enough to carry on personal correspondence with relatives and friends. She did her own shopping with money earned in baby-sitting, and she had now become the hostess in her home. She made it her personal responsibility to see that guests were made welcome.

She is still mentally retarded, but she recognizes her limitations, and is accepting and loving toward others. She moves freely and with confidence within her limited circle of friends and activities, and she is a contributing member in her home and community. The soul-searching over teaching methods, the patience, and the prayers were well worth the effort when the results are considered.

David's story is different. He had been graduated from high school but was essentially unable to read and write. It wasn't because he and his teachers hadn't cared or tried. Many of them had worked extra hours with him on their own, but without success. He never gave up hope, however, and each fall he would say, "This will be the year! This time somebody will teach me to read." But the years went on, and it didn't happen. David says even now he is sure he could observe the children in a schoolroom for five or ten minutes and tell those who can't read without ever hearing them say a word. How? Because he knows all the ways to "sit in a classroom and fill in time without getting in trouble." He spent twelve years filling in time.

With graduation from high school he set about building himself a life that didn't require reading. He was resourceful and learned the basic operation of earth moving equipment by watching day after day as a man operated his machine. He begged a chance to show the man what he had learned, and his ingenuity was rewarded. The fellow was impressed at David's handling of the equipment, and at the fact that he had memorized the function of the dials and levers and gauges because of his inability to read. He taught David the refinements of the skill and employed him.

David found ways to compensate in other areas of life, too, but was always on guard to conceal his reading problem because he felt ashamed of it. When he and a young college student became interested in each other, he leveled with her about his situation. Although her own attempt to teach him ended in frustration for both of them, she recognized his basically adequate intelligence and encouraged him to have himself tested to verify it. When the psychologist advised them that David's intelligence was, indeed, above average, she set about to find help for him. She met discouragement with every attempt but became so incensed that she refused to give up when a college professor expressed the opinion that if David had spent twelve years in school without learning to read he must be either too dumb or too lazy.

By this time my husband and I had developed a test for the auditory perceptual dysfunction which seemed to be such a critical factor in these cases of reading/spelling or speech/language disability. When David was finally referred to us we could tell him that his performance on our test indicated a severe dysfunction in auditory conceptualization. There was a high probability that if he worked with us and was successful in developing this ability to judge the number, identity, and sequence of sounds within a syllable he would then be able to learn to read and write. He couldn't believe it but agreed to one last try, expecting to convince his fiancée that his case was hopeless. In less than a year he was reading high school level material. It was hard work, but he *could* read, and his comprehension was good.

We had focused on the reading with a delayed approach to the writing, because of the limited amount of time available. David left for work before five in the morning and didn't get home until after eight in the evening. Then a new development occurred. Before we could make a concentrated effort on the writing, the Army drafted him. He had previously been rejected for illiteracy. He is back now, and ready to begin work on his writing. He says he feels as if he is a completely different person than he was when he couldn't read. It is as if he has been given a whole new life. Perhaps there is more than one way that a person can be born again.

Our test and the developmental/remedial program which emerged as we worked with these people and many others is now published. We find an increasing demand on our time for teaching teachers through university courses and inservice training in school districts. Our approach embodies concepts from my field of speech pathology and my husband's field of linguistics—disciplines in which most teachers have very little background. In addition to this, our research indicates that—similar to the general population—approximately 30 percent of the teachers we work with have some degree of auditory perceptual dysfunction themselves. They have compensated enough to "get by" in their own reading and spelling, but they cannot work effectively with a student's perceptual dysfunction until they have a base of perceptual competency themselves. For this reason it is a double challenge to be doing this teaching of teachers. It requires the same continual soul-searching and analysis of our teaching methods as does the work with students, and there is even more burden of responsibility with it. Each teacher will in turn be a force in hundreds of other lives. The effect of what we accomplish, or don't accomplish, with each teacher will be compounded many times.

There is often opportunity to witness, when working with teachers, that incredible as it seems God knows us as individuals and cares about the problems we face. As we draw from the source of infinite patience and wisdom, we will work in a different climate and with different skill than is otherwise possible. We have received verification from teachers of the Spirit which accompanied this witness and the stimulation and encouragement it provided. Many have also, in turn, shared with us a witness from their own reachings and the help they have received. And so the Lord's purposes in man are accomplished, that we witness one to another.

* * *

Here is the story of a man who also found great rewards through giving service in teaching. Wilbert Hayden gave up the security of a good job in industry to become a teacher in the first junior college in Canada located on the Blackfoot Indian Reserve fifty miles east of Calgary.

After working for twenty-eight years with Renfrew Chrysler as a mechanic and service manager, I became very bored listening to complaints about cars' rattles and decided to heed the theme of my pastor's handbook, "Venture with God into New Frontiers." When the opportunity presented itself to become an instructor in farm mechanics at Mount Royal College Old Sun Campus (Siksika), I accepted the challenge.

My friends wondered how I could leave the security of a good job, but when I asked God to assist me in my decision he helped me to see the insecurity of life itself in the loss of close friends who had built for retirement but did not live to enjoy the fruits of their hard work. Also I had come to know something of the problems of the Indian people who try to fit into white society. Helping them to make better lives for themselves seemed more important than acquiring an abundance of "things" that I might never live to use.

I have just finished my second year of teaching—two of the most thrilling years of my life. The first year there were eighteen young men in the farm mechanics class, and this past year twenty-four. I learned to know and love these people. One of the first things I discovered was that they don't need money nearly as much as they need to learn stewardship and learning the white man's ways isn't as important as their gaining the feeling of equal worth in the eyes of God and man.

My greatest thrill has been seeing young men recognize their abilities once they were given the right knowledge and tools. Let me use one illustration of a young married man with five children.

When Billy came to my class two years ago I was told he was an unreliable drunk. I watched him closely and after two months I could see the pattern of his behavior. Whenever he made a mistake he would miss a few days of class. I found that he believed what was being said about him . . . that he was just another drunken Indian. As I worked closely with him he began to develop confidence in himself and started correcting his mistakes instead of running away from them. When he successfully overhauled two tractors and two car motors, he felt the thrill of accomplishment. Billy has now completed fourteen months of working for a farm machinery dealer and has moved his family to a small town near the reserve along with another student and his family. Fifteen people have been taken from the welfare roll, but—more important—a man has experienced the thrill of being worth something.

As I write this, the police are dredging the Bow River for the bodies of four Indian boys who drove over the bank on the reserve. All were less than eighteen years old. They had learned white man's ways too well—how to use alcohol and how to abuse themselves. It seems to me that we, as Christians, should become more concerned about teaching our Indian friends of Christ's ways than our ways. To do this may take courage and imagination and perhaps sacrifice. But maybe it's time we became more concerned with people than with our own comfort or our own bank accounts.

* * *

Better education, both academic and practical, is a pressing need in many of the underdeveloped countries around the world. Schoolteachers and administrators can help develop better facilities and methods through government programs of foreign aid such as Point IV and its successor the Peace Corps. However, as Rolla Amsberry found, it takes a combination of patience, tact, and a strong constitution to provide this service in some of the more rugged areas of the world.

I well recall the baffled feeling we experienced when we arrived in Iran. We had come to give technical assistance in developing an educational program and found that most of the local educators were satisfied with their efforts and felt no need for a change. We knew that our innovations had to be worked into and through the program of the government's Department of Education. The problem was that the officials were quite willing to accept our financial help but were skeptical of our methods of education.

Such reservations were understandable. I knew how I would have felt if a total stranger from a foreign country had come to me when I was superintendent of an Iowa school and told me how to do my job. I'm afraid that I would not have been able to cover my resentment or to have been as gracious as Mr. Mostafa Zamani, General Director of the Khorasan Department of Education, was to me. During the next two years as we jockeyed for position, Mr. Zamani and I developed a place for each other in the educational field without loss of face by either of us. It became not only a business and professional relationship of mutual respect but also a friendship which I hold in high regard.

The problems of the first six months' work ran together

as a sort of extended nightmare: conferences, trips in a jeep over camel trails, rides on donkey back, walking, lack of water.

Finally out of the chaos, the first demonstration school was completed. My wife was put in charge, and Mr. Zamani provided a fine staff of teachers to be trained. The added enthusiasm of Mr. Nasser Azad, principal, permitted a real program of technical assistance to begin development.

However, it was still evident that Mr. Zamani felt there were two separate programs—theirs and ours. Somehow we had to integrate them . . . but how? The problem was clearly one of winning the acceptance and cooperation of the Iranian educators. We would have to establish an atmosphere of mutual respect and confidence. They would have to feel assured that we simply wanted to help the indigent teachers do a better job of teaching, that we were not trying to revolutionize the whole school program. We had to find an existing need and meet it by showing their teachers *how* to put their own program into action, . . . not by foisting American solutions on them. In other words, we had to prove that we had something important to give them if they were willing to work with us.

Our chance came in an area that was of tremendous importance to Iran. Because over 90 percent of the people were illiterate, the teaching of reading and writing was a primary concern of Iranian educators. Phonics had been taught in the schools but failed. It should have succeeded because the Iranian language (called Farsi) is almost 100 percent phonetic. In the demonstration school my wife had learned enough of the language to read part of the text. She demonstrated to Mr. Azad and the first grade teacher how the phonetic system should be taught. As an example she used the Farsi word for water . . . "ab." She wrote "ab" on the chalkboard and pronounced the word by its phonetic sounds "ah-ba." Mr. Azad's eyes were wide open as he exclaimed, "That's it, Mrs. Amsberry, that's it!" Then he explained that they had tried to use phonics, but instead of giving the sounds of the letters they had used the names of the letters—*aleph bey*—and that wasn't the way "ab" should be pronounced.

The use of this simple technique was the key that unlocked the teaching of Farsi reading and writing, thereby helping to combat illiteracy. It was also our breakthrough in persuading educators at all levels that we were there to help them with their problems and not to sabotage their system.

We set up experimental night schools in areas of the Ostan Province to be taught by the local teachers who had been trained at the demonstration school. Using the phonetic method adult peasants were able to learn to read and write within a few months. The students, adults, and children who had to work during the day and were unable to attend regular classes wouldn't miss a night. In fact, when the teacher did not show up on Friday (the Muslim holy day), the adults walked to the county seat early the next morning to protest to the Chief of Education. As a result, adult classes were held even on holy days.

When I visited some of the adult schools I was surprised and touched by the enthusiasm of the students. I had been asked to speak to the assembled classes, but the men kept interrupting me to express their pride and appreciation for their new accomplishments: "Just a few weeks ago we couldn't read or write. Now see what we can do!" As we left any spectator would have thought I was the Shah himself from the respectful way I was treated.

I asked the students to write a newsletter to me each week. They were to place one copy of it on the bulletin board in the village center and send one copy to the Chief of Education. Each week as I received my copy, I could just imagine the pride these people must have felt when they read their letter to friends gathered around the bulletin board.

Gradually we began to feel that members of the Department of Education were beginning to accept us as part of their own program rather than alien to it. In January Mr. Zamani visited the demonstration school along with a party of reporters from Tehran. As he observed the changed attitude of the teachers and pupils toward learning, he commented, "So this is what you mean by technical assistance!" In midsummer he told us, "Whatever, in your judgment, you think we should do, we'll do it."

In the fall the Ostan rural supervisors came to our office for advice. Our staff set up a workshop to teach them how to train the teachers of the rural schools and how to prepare teaching aids. At the close of this workshop, these supervisors asked if we would train all the Meshed regional supervisors. We did.

The final accolade for our efforts came from the chief of the Meshed Education Department. "Our program is your program," he told us cordially, "and yours is ours. Feel free to attend any meetings we may have without waiting for an invitation."

It isn't always easy to help people without causing waves of resentment. We felt that, at least, we had found the *how*.

Mona M. Goddard tells of her experiences working with the Title I program in a ghetto school.

* * *

> *As He died to make men holy*
> *Let us die to make men free,*
> *His truth is marching on.*

When I hear these words I get a lump in my throat that I never experienced before the four and a half years that I was a teacher aide in the Kansas City school system. My job was to work in the classroom assisting the teacher by relieving her of nonteaching duties and reinforcing her presentation of lessons.

I'll never again be able to say the pledge of allegiance to the flag—especially the words "with liberty and justice for all"—without thinking of the Negro children with whom I worked. Being in the ghetto is like being in a different world. The speech, actions, and thoughts of the people who live there are so different that it takes time, patience, love, and a sincere desire to be accepted to be able to serve effectively.

I was one of the first to work in the Title I pilot program in Kansas City. I was assigned to a school in the center of the deprived area. Never before had I known or worked with blacks. I knew how white children in my area treated Negro teachers (very disrespectfully) and I wondered if I would receive the same kind of treatment. As I walked in the door and sat down with the rest of the aides awaiting room assignments I could feel the tension and apprehension of the other aides in the room.

I was assigned to an all-black third grade class with a Negro teacher who was in her first year of teaching. She was unsure of herself and really did not know what to do with another adult. The project was developed so quickly that the teachers had been notified only the night before that theirs was to be one of the schools that had been chosen for the pilot program.

As I walked into the room the children looked at me as if to say, "What are you doing here? Go away!" I came to learn that the children in these deprived areas are very attached to their teachers, who may represent the only stable element in their lives. As they began to accept me, I found I could hold them, help them, and love them. Eventually they even came to me with their troubles.

Everything went smoothly until one day on the playground a fight started, and I had to intervene. When this happened one of the boys turned to me and started shouting. "You can't make me stop. . . . I don't have to mind you. Don't you dare touch me!" In that moment it seemed that everything which had been building up inside of him poured out. He was one of a very large family and often stayed up half the night roaming the streets because he had no sleeping space at home. Most of the food he ate was what he received free at school, and if he was late or misbehaved even this was denied him. He was the bully of the playground and signed himself "Leonard the King." As shown by the incident on the playground, he seemed to have a deep hatred for me, but since I was assigned to work with the slow ones he had no choice but to be under my tutelage. Slowly, with the extra attention I gave him, he began to become interested in reading. When he finally learned to read a simple story a new light came to his eyes. He'd done something everyone else was doing!

Many times during the next few years I was to hear the words, "You make me sick" . . . and when I asked, "Why?" I was told, "because you're white." I was also told, "I don't want to be black. Why did God make me black and you white?"

The next fall I was assigned to Woodland School. I began the year with a little more confidence and again was assigned to assist new teachers—one Negro and one white. Working with the Negro teacher, making home telephone calls, talking with Negro parents, and working with the home school coordinator, I began to understand the problems of the children. Some were of their own making; some were born of prejudice and ignorance; and some came of circumstances beyond their control.

I developed great respect for the teachers and aides I

worked with. One Negro teacher had provided a foster home for thirty-three children from the juvenile department; only four of these were black. Despite the no prayer rule in the public schools, many of the black teachers had the children ask a blessing on the food either in their rooms, in the hall, or at the table before they ate.

One day while eating lunch with the other aides I learned of racial prejudice on another level. One young woman was holding down two jobs trying to save money to buy a home in a better neighborhood. She was told a certain house was available until the agent discovered she was black. Then it turned out the house had already been sold. She tried for a job at a place that advertised equal employment but was told by the employer that he didn't make a habit of hiring Negroes because they were unreliable. The hurt went deep.

As I listened to the musical program at which the seventh and eighth graders stood up and sang "Mine eyes have seen the glory of the coming of the Lord . . . as he died to make men holy, let us die to make men free" I realized they were singing from their hearts of their fears and hopes. I silently thanked God for giving me the privilege to work with these—a part of his people.

Even though I am no longer with the Title I Program, my thoughts and prayers go with others who work with it. I well remember the hands that reached out to me, the arms that went around my neck, and the times those students came to me when they were hurt and bewildered. These are things that money cannot buy and time cannot fade.

Being housemother of a dormitory is a unique way of serving young people. It sometimes presents problems, not the least of which is being accepted by the students.

[27] At a women's meeting in 1957 the guest speaker challenged me to do some real thinking about my life and job. She said that God put all of us here for a purpose and if we didn't know what our purpose was, it was because we weren't sufficiently concerned and didn't pray enough.

After leaving that meeting I decided to really pray that if God had a work for me to do the way would open for me and I would know for myself. I had a good job with excellent pay, but the more I thought the more I was convinced that it wasn't benefitting anyone but me.

Shortly after this our women's group leader went into the hospital for surgery. A few days after her operation she called me to come to see her; she said she had something important to tell me. When I went to visit her that afternoon she told me that she had been praying for me and she knew there was a job for me there at the hospital.

A few days later I was asked to put in my application at the bank where a bookkeeper would be needed as soon as some remodeling was finished. While this was going on, the head housemother at the Nurses' Dormitory called and asked if I would like to be a housemother for the student nurses. I was surprised and asked what the requirements were. When she said there were none I laughingly told her I should be able to handle that.

I went in that afternoon for an interview with the Director of Nursing. I wasn't at all sure I wanted to be a housemother, but I prayed as I walked to the hospital that I would be able to know for sure whether this was the job God wanted me to take.

Almost the first thing Miss Morgan said to me was, "You are an answer to my prayer." I was shocked, but even this didn't entirely convince me that I was supposed to take the job. She told me that in salary I would be taking a big cut from what I had been getting. At that moment the pay wasn't a major concern—I just wanted to be sure that in taking this job I would be truly in God's service.

Miss Morgan asked me to go to the dorm that evening to learn more about the job. On my way there many thoughts went through my mind: What about the bookkeeping job at the bank? How would the girls accept me—particularly the ones from Hawaii? How would I accept them? I decided if we didn't hit it off that night I would not stay.

I walked through the hospital to the tunnel leading to the dorm. It was dingy and dark. I hesitated, thinking, I can't believe this is for me! However, as I started to walk through I was engulfed with a beautiful Spirit, and my feet didn't feel as if they ever touched the floor. There was no longer any doubt in my mind. I said, "God, this has to be it."

The first girl who greeted me in the dorm was Sukie from Hawaii. She was so sweet and so happy to meet me that we became friends on the spot. There were thirty-three seniors, thirty-eight juniors, and forty-three freshmen to greet me; they came from nearly every state in the United States including Hawaii, from Canada, and even one from South Vietnam. I loved them all.

I became the night housemother and stayed until the curriculum was changed to a four-year program and the dorm was discontinued. When it was over I looked back on thirteen wonderful years and the greatest field of service I had ever known.

Milton Broadfoot's vocation gives him special opportunities to give worthwhile service to young people.

For nearly twenty-five years I have been an educational representative and executive director of the Iowa Council on

Alcohol Problems. This nonprofit church-oriented organization sponsors a teaching program concerning the physical effects of alcohol on the body. Our program is geared for the junior and senior high schools in Iowa, and the thrust of the effort is "An ounce of prevention is worth a pound of cure."

As an alcohol education specialist I have lectured before thousands of young people. I try to remember before I enter a classroom or assembly hall to offer a silent petition for the help of the Good Spirit in my presentation. Many times I have experienced that Spirit of ministry in working with these youth. From time to time principals and teachers have come to me when I have finished my assignment in a school saying that they have heard many assembly speakers but there was something "different"—a special quality—in my effort.

If with the Master's help I can convince even one young person in each group of the rightness of the total abstinence way of life I shall feel that my efforts are indeed worthwhile.

The functions of a minister naturally present opportunities for special service. A truly dedicated servant of God will find himself rendering service that goes far beyond the bounds of the traditional functions of preaching, baptizing, and visiting.

Men like Dr. Ray Fedje are effective in social ministry aimed at young people. Other needs can also be served.

Consider the ministers who are doing premarital and marital counseling as part of their job; arranging for old people to get into rest homes or convalescent centers; helping families plan their finances by budgeting; comforting bereaved families; and counseling people who are physically or emotionally ill.

So far the service opportunities mentioned in this chapter have been the type that grow directly out of specific vocations. However, there are also opportunities for service which are related to or grow indirectly out of paid vocations.

Many doctors, nurses, and dentists donate weeks or even months of their time and skills in remote parts of the world. An example of this is the Missions Health Foundation which sends medical teams to areas where little or no health care is available. Under its auspices several teams serve annually in Haiti and Honduras. Often these people work in the mountainous, jungle areas of the interior where they must travel by jeep, mule, and on foot. Composed of doctors of medicine and dentistry, nurses, technicians, and assistants, these professional teams (serving at their own expense) have aided thousands of Haitians and Hondurans. Their primary work has been in the field of immunization, acute treatment, dental care, and health education.

Often a person of the medical profession will give volunteer service on medical missions after retirement. Such a one is Christena Turner who has served in Honduras for six years. Not only has she functioned in her own capacity as a nurse but also extracted teeth.

Sometimes a casual service can bring its own reward in unexpected ways.

One day a woman without an appointment came into the dental office of Dr. Ray James. She was in considerable distress, a stranger in town, and almost without funds. She had had a tooth extracted in another city and the socket was now bleeding. Dr. James sutured and packed it. In the course of conversation he learned that she had just been released from a tuberculosis sanitarium. Knowing that she could not have had time to get a job, he told her there would be no charge for his services. A few days later he received a letter from her asking him to trace his hand on a piece of paper and send it to her. He did so, mystified and intrigued as to why she wanted him to do this. Later he received a handsome pair of handmade gloves that fit perfectly. This was a craft taught to patients in the sanitarium, and she had used her skill to "exchange services" with the man who had used his skill to help her.

People of imagination and concern can find extra opportunities for service in almost any vocation.

An accountant may serve as volunteer treasurer or auditor for church groups, service organizations, and charity foundations.

A building contractor can use his know-how and equipment to design, supervise, and build for church projects. A fine example of this type of service is Charles Bickel who has given holidays and weekends of unpaid service to supervise construction of a church camping facility in southern Indiana. Men skilled in various building trades have also acted as volunteers—electricians, carpenters, heavy equipment operators. And there has been much unskilled labor donated also. All of this has been coordinated and drawn together into a smooth operation by Bickel. His ability to estimate the needs for building materials and buy them at the best possible prices was an economic help also.

Professional musicians can use their talent to serve others and give pleasure. They can sing or play instruments for church services or special programs. Many members and former members of a London, Ontario, congregation retain enduring memories of fine worship experiences provided by the church orchestra. Made up of amateur musicians, many of whom later became professionals, the orchestra accompanied the congregational singing and provided special music every Sunday morning. Trained musicians can also help with youth work in vacation church schools and youth camps.

Actors can direct and act in church plays. Along with musicians, such "show business" people frequently find a great deal of personal satisfaction in giving benefit performances or making personal appearances for medical foundations and charitable organizations. These volunteer appearances should not be negated as "ego trips," for many of these performers sincerely desire to use their talents to serve others.

Cooks, dietitians, and home economists can use their knowledge and training in the food service for family and youth camps, retreats, day care centers, congregational dinners, church banquets, and fund raising meals. They also can give much needed service in low-income areas teaching homemakers about nutritional needs and wise buying.

Project Shampoo was a rather offbeat outgrowth of teaching. Several junior high girls from low-income homes had become quite offensive with their lack of personal hygiene. Their clothing smelled of perspiration and was seldom changed; their hair was like rats' nests, and their teeth were rotting. Their idea of taking a shower after P.E. class was, if absolutely forced, to walk as quickly as possible across the outer edge of the shower so they wouldn't get wet. Four of the women teachers decided to try to help them help themselves.

The girls were promised new hairstyles . . . just like the movie stars! That began it. Shampoo, towels, curlers, and hair dryers were collected. Two of the teachers supervised the showers, and at the beginning one of the teachers had to "go the third mile" by getting into the shower with the girls and showing them how to get their hair really clean. Back in their clothes again, the girls were taken to the teachers' lounge where the other two teachers showed them how to put their hair up on rollers to achieve the style they had picked. Another teacher stayed with them while they sat under the dryers, then helped them comb their hair into the desired styles. Incidentally, the teachers involved gave up their preparation period for the day in order to work with these girls.

Probably a more usual extra service open to teachers lies in the personal counseling of students.

* * *

[28] Tears were streaming down his hollow cheeks as he begged, "Help me . . . please help me!" He reached out toward me, and sobs shook his thin frame. He was so weak I had to support him as he walked around the small hospital room. "Why won't they just let me die?" he cried.

The young man was a drug addict. He had lost his job and had a marriage that was crumbling around him. I had been called to his bedside at the Western Mental Health Clinic. As I sat by his bedside after he had finally calmed down and was sleeping restlessly, my mind drifted back to the tow-headed youth I had met six years before. He was fifteen years old at the time and was a student in the school where I taught. Little did I know or could I have imagined at that time how stormy the next six years would be for him. His first fifteen years had been nightmarish enough. He was the product of a broken home and had spent his childhood being shifted around—unwanted by either parent. Even at fifteen, the lack of love had left deep scars on him. Somehow, a friendship began between us as he felt that I cared for him as a person and learned that he could trust me.

Many times over the six years that followed, he came to me for advice or just to talk. He seldom followed my advice, but somehow, strangely, when he was troubled, he would show up—sometimes wild-eyed and high, sometimes weeping uncontrollably, sometimes excited about some new project which was nearly always impractical. I always listened and then counseled him. Many times the advice I gave was not to his liking and so, frankly, I was surprised each time he returned. Seeing his life continue on its downhill course, I had decided that this was one of my failures. As I sat by his bedside I wondered, after six unsuccessful years, what I could possibly do now.

Fortunately God has given me a special love and concern for young people. Perhaps it is this love that they feel and turn to. I had always talked to this young man as I do to all I counsel about God and how His influence can change their lives and strengthen them. I can testify of this, because I was converted as an adult, and I know the power God has to change lives. He changed mine! Perhaps the fact that I spent my youth apart from him and made many mistakes makes me more understanding and patient. With this young man, however, I had nearly lost hope. Then he said, "You talk to Him for me, will you?" Somewhere, through the depths of his despair, he was trying to reach to God through me. Then I realized that I was merely an instrument. I could witness of divine love and forgiveness, but only through God himself could this young man be saved.

Before I left him that night he pressed into my hand a crumpled piece of paper which read:

> Here I am God, praying again . . . asking you to help
> me find my way.
> Please help me, dear God, I hurt so bad inside.
> Oh please God, there's got to be a better way . . .
> 'Cause I am lonely and all mixed up in my mind . . .
> please tell me I've caught myself in time.

I cannot explain what happened, but God moved and the hurt inside was lessened, and the lonely space was filled with warmth and love. In a few weeks, this young man walked into my office. He looked like a new person. His shaking and stuttering had stopped, and he was looking for work. He was off drugs and was receiving professional counseling regularly. He had moved, was avoiding his old friends, and was making new ones who were a good influence. He said he didn't know life could be like this. His despair had changed to hope.

When he reached out to God, God was there—as He always is. As long as my young friend can keep his hand in the hand of God, he will make it.

Over my fifteen years in public education and youth work I have met and worked with all kinds of young people. Through God and his Holy Spirit, I have been able to understand their needs, their dreams, and their problems. God, through his love in my life, has given me the capacity to love them in spite of their faults. Because I care, they somehow seem to sense that care and come to me. There have been some failures, but it still has been worth all the effort.

The time seems so short during which I can influence these young people. When they graduate, there is an empty place in my life and a time of wondering . . . "Have I done enough? Have I said the right things? Have I been an acceptable instrument for God?" . . . But then there is always another student waiting who needs to know that someone cares about him, someone who will take time to listen.

A nurse, Mrs. Ella Winholtz, was forced by ill health to retire from full-time nursing. As she became stronger she offered her assistance in volunteer service such as in summer camp nursing and teaching classes for the American Red Cross. It was during one of her volunteer assignments that she began a service project which has spanned several years and drastically changed a life.

* * *

In the summer of 1966 I was asked to relieve the nurse who had been hired for the summer at Camp Doniphan. Since it amounted to only two days a week and consisted mainly of supervising and teaching student nurses, it was not too difficult for me. It was here that I met Marcie.

From the start I knew that she was a very lonely, emotionally disturbed girl. She spent a great deal of time with me in the First Aid room those two days, telling me about her life in great detail. Among other things she told me that she had had psychiatric care for several years, had left her home in a small town and moved to Kansas City at the age of seventeen. Also she had spent some time in various foster homes. When my two days were completed at camp that week, Marcie asked me if she could have my phone number and permission to call me when she wanted to. I gladly gave her both.

That fall she returned to Metropolitan Junior College. The school year was a rough one for her—emotionally and financially. The most stabilizing factor in her life was a conscientious and concerned school counselor who spent much time and effort trying to keep the girl on the right track. Even so she had difficulty stretching her small welfare check to cover room rent, food, clothing, and other necessities. Her health was in jeopardy because of improper eating and she never had enough for the kind of clothing she needed. This made it difficult for her to maintain self-respect.

Eventually she began keeping company with kids who got their kicks out of alcohol and drugs. I was convinced that this type of life was foreign to the person she really wanted to be, but she seemed unable to break away from these friends.

As time went on, her problems increased. Although she was an intelligent girl, she was "just squeaking by" in some of her subjects. As spring approached, my husband and I became convinced that the only way we could really help

Marcie was to have her come to live with us. We knew it was a risk. Because of her emotional instability she would not be able to stand another rejection if we invited her into our home and then the whole relationship blew up. I consulted people I felt were competent to advise us and their advice was that this would be a mistake—she was too far gone to be helped. Since I like challenges, I was all the more certain that we should at least make an attempt to help her.

By this time Marcie had gotten involved with the National Council on Alcoholism. She proved to be more psychologically than physically addicted, and she found people there she could trust as friends without the necessity of drinking. Also at this time she was going to the clinic at General Hospital two or three times a week for migraine headaches and various other complaints. Many times she would receive a "shot" for pain and be sent home with a new supply of medicine. She soon accumulated a considerable supply of pain pills, barbiturates, and tranquilizers.

Ten days before Marcie was to come to live with us she took an overdose of drugs. As a result of the commotion that she caused, her landlady who lived in the house and was ill ordered her to move. When I arrived, I found her deeply sedated and discovered that the school counselor who had helped her before had arranged to have her taken to the hospital in conjunction with Suicide Prevention and the Mental Health Center. Plans also had been formulated to have her transferred to the State Hospital.

I immediately suggested an alternate plan to the school counselor. I asked for permission to take Marcie to our home when she was dismissed by the Mental Health Center. Permission was granted provided I would meet the counselor there at 8:00 a.m. since Marcie was not to be released to anyone but her.

On Monday morning we waited in the front lobby for her

to be brought down from her room. What a sad sight she was! Two people had to support her as she came down the stairs and sat down in a chair next to a table where she immediately laid her head to continue sleeping. In addition to her general pathetic appearance, Marcie had seventy-nine self-inflicted cigarette burns. A well-meaning employee had supplied the cigarette, not realizing what it would be used for.

As we waited to have her dismissal processed, the doctor in charge came to see us. Observing her condition, he suggested that she be left in the hospital for a few more days to allow the sedation to wear off. We readily agreed.

When we took Marcie home the latter part of the week she was a very apprehensive, frightened girl, but she seemed happy at the prospect of having a home and family. Three days later she was dismissed from psychiatric group therapy. She told us that the doctor's parting comment to her was that she was impossible and incorrigible.

The first few months were quite an adjustment for her and for us. We talked openly together about the things we expected of her and what she could expect from us. As far as rules went, we decided to make them only when the need arose.

Although Marcie appreciated finding a home and a loving family, she had not yet learned to communicate reciprocal love. She often tested us to see if our love and concern were genuine or if, somehow, there might have been some other motive for us to want her to live with us.

As we worked with Marcie on her problems we stressed that she must take the responsibility for her own actions. She seemed very afraid at first, and we tried to help by letting her know that she had our support and love.

One thing that we could not accept was her undesirable behavior when she was "upset." We would not tolerate her using this as an excuse. Her first "shock treatment" in this respect happened when she had been with us about a week. Following some very bizarre behavior of hers I firmly announced, "You're not 'crazy' and I don't expect you to act that way, so you had better straighten up and fly right." (Later she told me how delighted she was to hear this, after having been led to believe otherwise for so long.)

Some aspects of her childhood had been very unpleasant, and Marcie had developed a compulsive desire to talk about it. I believed this was not conducive to good mental health and discouraged it. I assured her that we were interested in her past problems, but we felt it was of no value to her to continually review them. She was not forbidden to mention her past, but I encouraged her to refrain from repetitious accounts and suggested that she concentrate on what she planned to do in the future. Gradually the things which had so filled her mind became less important and she began to regard her past as a bad dream.

Another thing which was most evident at first but gradually disappeared was her fear of rejection. This was especially obvious when we differed in opinion or if she did something which she was quite sure might not please us. When she first moved in, she was like a frightened kitten and seldom came near us. As she gained confidence, she became very close and appeared starved for affection. This led to a new complication. Marcie felt very threatened when our own daughter would show up at our home. Finally I asked Barbara, without letting Marcie know it, to make her calls a little less often for a while in order to give Marcie more time to adjust. Eventually the two girls developed an excellent relationship.

Perhaps the major problem was drugs. As I mentioned earlier, Marcie had a large supply—including dilantin and phenobarbital—when she arrived at our home. When the authorities at the Mental Health Center dismissed her they had given her instructions not to take anything except a mild headache medicine which they gave her. A complete physical checkup with our family doctor resulted in the same advice. Yet periodically we saw unmistakable signs that she was using drugs.

We knew that it was very important physically and emotionally for her to get off drugs as soon as possible, but with several large bottles of various kinds in her possession we wondered if she could refrain from taking them. Again we said that the responsibility was hers. She was entitled to her privacy and we would not snoop in her room, but we hoped she would get rid of her unneeded supply of drugs. When she continued to use them I applied a little more pressure, suggesting that she give the remaining medicine to me. She complied—partially.

It was the latter part of the summer when I confronted her for the last time about the matter. As she handed a few more pills to me, she asked if I would believe her if she told me she was giving me all she had. I said, "Yes, I'll believe you." It was never necessary to bring up the subject again. We realized, of course, that when she went back to school she would be able to get drugs easily if she wanted them; however, as far as we know she never betrayed our trust.

That fall she went back to Metropolitan Junior College. Her condition had improved tremendously and she had begun to take a great deal of pride in her grooming. Even her body carriage revealed her new self-confidence.

During this period she returned to the Health Center to visit a friend who worked there and found that a doctor who had worked with her did not recognize her. He was so pleased with the change that he sent for a second doctor who had felt that she showed little promise. This doctor asked how she accounted for the change, and Marcie answered, "The only thing I can think of is that I have parents who let me love them, and I have a mother who puts the responsibility on my own shoulders for everything I do." This visit was an extra boost to her morale.

During the latter part of the fall semester Marcie felt a strong urge to enter the health field as an occupational therapist. Since she was very talented with her hands and had shown so much determination, we encouraged her to pursue this profession. Although her academic record at Metropolitan had been poor, the University of Kansas finally agreed to accept her on probation for the spring semester. With a certain amount of apprehension, she went into one of the dormitories on the campus to start this new phase of her life.

Feeling that she had an opportunity to get an education in the field of her own choosing (and being desirous of proving a great many people wrong who had said she couldn't reach her goal) she worked very hard and by mid-semester had made the honor roll. In fact as she was prone to do, she worked almost too hard for her own good, putting all the physical and emotional strength she had into her studies. It proved to be too much for her. About three weeks before school was out that spring my husband and I joined our daughter and son-in-law on a ten-day vacation. All her old feelings of insecurity and loneliness returned, and she resorted to some of her former bizarre behavior and cut her arm.

She was taken to the campus hospital and physically recovered quickly. Of course, it was disappointing to us to see her come so near to "blowing it," but all we could do was to let her know that she still had our support and love.

The doctor who attended her seemed to understand her emotional problems quite well and arranged for her to attend class and remain at the hospital at all times outside of class. In this way she was able to finish the semester's work.

The university doctor and a consulting clinical psychologist tried to persuade me that it would be foolish to let her attempt to finish college. I could not agree. Because of her complete exhaustion it was necessary for Marcie to stay out of school that summer and rest, but when the fall semester began our family doctor gave his consent for her to enroll.

Within the first month there was more trouble. Her roommate was a girl with less than the highest morals. Things went bad for Marcie when she requested a room change and subsequently reported to the girl in charge of their floor that she thought she had found evidence of drug usage in their room. Such a serious report had to go to the house mother and then on to the Dean of Women.

Ironically, it was Marcie herself who came under suspicion rather than her roommate. After all, she was the one who had had psychiatric problems. The police searched the room, and although nothing was found in Marcie's possessions the Dean of Women made an appointment for a conference with us. There was not much discussion because the Dean and the house mother had already decided that Marcie could no longer stay in the dorm. They did not come to the point of saying that she could not remain in the school, but they did not encourage us to leave her there. We found out later that her being able to stay and continue her studies was due in large part to the efforts of the junior college counselor who had so valiantly stood by Marcie in the past.

When Marcie was called into the conference, I saw the old "whipped pup" expression on her face that I had not seen since her arrival in our home almost a year and a half before. After being ousted from the dorm, she commuted from home—a hundred-mile round trip. Usually I drove her to school in the morning, and she caught a bus or sometimes a ride home with other students from our area. In spite of the tempestuous events of the semester, she again came through on the honor roll.

The next two semesters went along very smoothly, with Marcie working hard at her studies as well as growing stronger emotionally. This time she made the dean's list, being at the top of her class in all subjects except one.

Her first affiliation was a three-month period in a psychiatric hospital in Connecticut. We could have felt a great deal of apprehension about this, but we were not unduly concerned—and obviously neither was she. By this time she had gained a lot of self-confidence and had apparently been strengthened by the reversals which she had met and overcome.

At the end of those three months she came home a winner. She completed her work there at the top of her class, and in the final report her director wrote a summary of the various instructors' opinions: "Marcie is a person that a director of any psychiatric institution would be proud to have in the department." This was an added triumph for Marcie. She felt that she had at last proved to herself and everyone else that she was no longer a patient but a therapist.

Following this came her last semester at the University, then a semester at the Kansas City Medical Center, and finally three more affiliations. The first was in Texas, the next in Nebraska, and the final one in Hawaii. Because of her good grades she had been given first choice of location for her affiliations and had been sent to Hawaii as a representative from the school. While in Hawaii on her last affiliation, she took the national exam which made her a registered occupational therapist.

After a few weeks rest at home, Marcie rented an apartment and obtained employment. She has worked steadily and successfully for over two years and is now employed in a private psychiatric hospital.

Although she is no longer living in our home, she continues to be very close to us. She is "one of our kids."

* * *

It takes special effort, but there are special rewards for those who go the second mile . . . and the third . . . and the fourth.

CHAPTER SEVEN

"What Color Is God's Skin?"

[29] When I was a child I was intrigued by missionaries with their slides, pictures, souvenirs, and stories about foreign countries. When I married, my husband shared this interest; we determined that someday we would serve our brothers who were not fortunate enough to live in a country as affluent and peaceful as our native Canada.

We know it sounds idealistic and naïve, but we talked about having an international family of twelve—some children of our own and some to be adopted from other lands. While we were still in college we saw a film on Korea showing the abandoned illegitimate children of servicemen, and we were deeply affected. With my mother's help we sponsored a little Korean boy through the Canadian Save the Children Fund. This meant providing $108 a year for his support, plus sending gifts, birthday money, clothes, and letters as often as we could.

Much as we enjoyed (and still enjoy) doing this, it wasn't enough. It lacked the personal touch. We wanted a baby in our home—to be loved and touched and watched as it grew.

Four years ago there was a front-page story in the *London Free Press* about a badly wounded Vietnamese girl. Her face, horribly scarred by shrapnel, stared out at us from the newspaper. Although we were not through university yet we decided we must do something to help such children.

Our first move was to contact our local Child Welfare and inquire how we could adopt a Vietnamese child. We were told that the idea was "federally impossible." It never had been done; it couldn't be done. (We knew from newspaper articles that it *was* being done in the United States.)

Since we were committed to go to Europe to teach for two years, we did not worry about our temporary problem. We felt that once in Europe we would be closer to the situation and would find some solution. Our visits to the Middle and Far East only intensified our interest, but inquiries to the Canadian Military Child Welfare Agent in Germany brought the same old answer: "It's federally impossible." We turned to the American military authorities and church agencies but received only discouragement: "You're out of your minds. You don't know what kind of mental and physical disabilities such a child might have . . . or the diseases it might bring with it."

When we returned to Canada we wrote to two American agencies. The authorities of one of these (the Holt Agency in Oregon) said they would be glad to get us a child from Korea, but there was no agency in Ontario they could work through to get the child admitted to the province. We went back to our local Child Welfare, and again we were told it was impossible.

Our pleading went unheeded, and we became discouraged. Almost convinced that there really was no way to accomplish our goal, we decided to begin a home study with the idea of adopting an interracial (part Negro, Indian, or Eskimo) child from Canada while seeking further information on foreign adoptions.

The breakthrough came two months later quite by accident. Coming out of school one night I saw a little West African boy riding his bike. A woman whom I recognized as the mother of one of my students came out of her front door at just that moment and in response to my question said that the boy was her adopted son. I immediately told her the story of our four-year struggle to adopt a foreign child and asked for her guidance. Two weeks later she gave us the address of the Families for Children Agency in Quebec which had just completed arrangements to get eleven children into Canada from Korea and other countries. In Quebec, unlike Ontario, there is no problem. It has private agencies, and the provincial government does not object to the adoptions of foreign children.

We called Families for Children in Montreal and set the machinery in motion to get our Vietnamese baby. Our local Child Welfare agent was aghast when we called to tell her of our success. Like our lawyer she spent some time trying to convince us of the horrors we were letting ourselves in for. We appreciated the concern but, although we were a bit frightened by the pessimism, we continued gathering the required papers and praying that we would find a child we could help.

About two weeks later we got a call from Montreal telling us about the emergency situation in Bangladesh and asking if we would be interested in taking a child from that country. The Reverend Fred Cappuccino and his wife, president of Families for Children, planned to go to Bangladesh in early July and bring back several babies. As we knew it would take six months to a year to get a child out of Vietnam, we decided we could take a little Bengali while we waited for our Vietnamese baby.

Once again we began gathering the necessary documents. Everything proceeded smoothly until we came to one item. We needed a letter stating that we had had a home study done and we were approved. Letters and telephone calls simply resulted in referrals from one government agency to another. Finally a deadline came up. The Bengali babies were in Canada, and we had to have our final permission from the Ontario government for the adoption of our baby by Thursday or she would go to someone else in another province. We could not bear the thought of losing her now that we had come this far.

On Wednesday—the day before the deadline—a provincial official, friendly to our cause, promised to contact Prime Minister Trudeau's office with a last-minute appeal for federal help. He also suggested a barrage of telegrams from people in our home area—church ministers, for example. I immediately began calling the ministers of London churches, and the results of the next few hours still seem like a miracle to me. Every minister was home on the first telephone call. Each listened to my twenty- to thirty-minute explanation and then agreed to send the telegram at his own expense and support our cause, thus committing himself to something that he really knew very little about.

The telegrams were sent Thursday morning. The Ontario governmental agency gave official permission that afternoon.

Amina, our beautiful little daughter, was one of seven Bengali babies allowed to enter Ontario at that time. It seems almost a miracle that these babies fitted into their new homes and families as though they had been matched. Despite the darker skin, they even resemble the adoptive parents in build, facial features, and personality. One boy looks like his new father; another is big-boned like both of his new parents; a third is little and quiet like the people who took him.

Canada is not free from racial prejudice, and many people still ask us why we have adopted a Bengalese baby who will no doubt face prejudice and discrimination as she grows up. True, Amina and others like her will find bigotry and hatred in many quarters, but this is nothing to what she would have had to endure had she remained in her own country. She, like so many of these little unwanted waifs, is a result of rape. In her country the mother was blamed. Her father was an enemy soldier, hated by the defeated people; this hatred would carry over to the child. Amina would not be accepted by her mother's family, therefore she would have no cast. There would be no one to care for her, provide the necessities of life, educate her, or arrange a marriage. She would forever be a nonperson in the country of her birth. Here she has a loving family, food, care, security, and education to prepare her for life. Surely with these things she will be able to face the unkindness of a few.

The late Pearl Buck is probably the most famous person to champion the cause of hard-to-place biracial children. During and after World War II she adopted or helped to place hundreds of Oriental babies fathered by white or black soldiers. The plight of these children—unacceptable to either race—has touched the hearts of Christians throughout the world. It is not surprising that Maureen and Bob Hines (see page 74) who reared some of her brothers, sister, nieces, and several foster boys, should have become interested in adopting biracial children.

When we applied for a child to adopt we decided to ask for one who didn't belong in either the "black world" or the "white world," because we knew it could belong to us.

What an experience we had finding Tiffany! We applied and were promptly shown five "histories." After much deliberation we decided to take a little three-year-old girl named Mary Jane. Pictures arrived, but we were anxious for the child, not mere pictures. Two months passed with only negative information—the little girl was sick, she wasn't adjusting well, she had stopped talking. During this time I started having second thoughts. Adoption was such a big step; we'd had our share of joys and sorrows with children; I was thirty-four—maybe too old to start with little ones—and perhaps we were choosing our own way, not God's. By the time our scheduled meeting with Mary Jane arrived, I was filled with doubts. But Bob wasn't—he knew it was right!

A social worker was to bring Mary Jane to a large shopping center in Toronto where we could observe her without her knowing. Then, if we decided it wouldn't work she would not feel rejected. We walked around for nearly an hour waiting for her to appear (I was ready to give up after ten minutes). Finally there she was, and it was love at first sight. No one else seemed to exist for those few minutes—no shoppers, no clerks, no social worker—just our little girl. The love that began that day is still growing. We renamed her Tiffany, and for us she is truly God's gift.

Derek came to us a year and three months later, and again there was the miracle of assurance that he belonged to us from the moment we met. Our love for him is beyond telling.

So now our family is five again—Susan, nearly fifteen; two foster boys—Rick, fourteen, and Joe, twelve; Tiffany, five; and Derek, two. I really believe that love multiplies as it is divided, and if there are more children who need us, we'll welcome them.

* * *

Priscilla and Dale Carrick can also testify of the joys and sorrows, problems and solutions of adopting biracial children.

In the spring of 1968 our church adult class was studying Roger Shinn's *Tangled World*. While discussing the chapter on racial problems I was appalled at the feelings expressed by our active church friends. When we suggested that we could accept Negro friends we were challenged with, "You just think you can." Although we live in a small town community which has but one Negro family, we knew of the problems existing in many cities. We went home from class asking, "God, what can we do?" Our prayer was that he would guide us to do something in our family to help alleviate negative black-white relationships.

It was at this time that we began to consider taking a black baby into our home—one small enough for people to touch and hold. In this way they might find out that blacks are human too. To make sure that this was not just some bright idea thought up out of our emotionalism, we decided to put it to a test. Knowing that taking a baby would alter our whole family structure and would also prevent my finishing college and then teaching, I had to be sure that we could manage. We talked it over with the children: Vicki 16, Susan 15, David 12, Cathy 11, Mark 8. All agreed, so I cared for a three-year-old for a month to see how we would fare with another child in our home. In addition to this, I believe I took care of more baby nieces and nephews during that month than I had in years. Surprisingly my work got done, I felt better than ever, and the whole family loved it.

Our next step was to check on agencies to see if we could keep a foster black baby. When we finally went to the Department of Social Services in our own county, we were asked if we had thought of adoption. Dale and I just looked at each other, grinned, and then explained that we already had five children. The caseworker said, "No problem"—the laws had just been changed two months previously to allow such adoptions. He also explained that the need was greatest at that time for biracial children, as neither black nor white families seemed to want them. So we applied for a black or biracial boy, three years old or younger.

Many things happened during the adoption process to make us feel that God was truly behind this venture.

Jonnie—a beautiful, friendly, happy child—quickly won his way into the hearts of even those who were at first cold toward him. He instinctively knew which people to run up to and which ones to charm at a distance in order to give them time to adjust.

In a very short time we realized that we would not be fair to Jonnie to bring him up alone. We were spoiling him shamefully . . . as was practically everyone with whom he came in contact. His heritage—three-fourths Negro, one-eighth Caucasian, and one-eighth Indian—made him look charmingly Latin. We again had a family council and decided to try to get him a baby sister.

After completing the adoption study we asked God to send us the child which he felt we could most help. No girls were available, but a little half Caucasian, half Negro boy was in dire need of a home. Bennie did not respond normally; in fact there was the possibility that he was so mentally retarded that he might need to be institutionalized eventually. Both of his parents were retarded, possibly because of their extremely deprived background environment. During his short life he had been in four foster homes. After we discussed with the children all of the possible complications of taking him, with unanimous approval we went to see Bennie. He calmly looked us over and sucked his thumb, with never a wiggle or a sound. Although he was almost a year old, he was tiny. The most striking thing about him was his big brown eyes.

When we got him about a month later he had been moved to another foster home and already was responding more normally. Now, at four, Benjamin Robert is the most active, alert, intelligent child I have ever seen.

How could we afford this financially? After we got Jonathon, and Vicki was ready to start college, we were able to sell enough gravel from an abandoned gravel pit which we had purchased to completely pay for Vicki's first two years. After we had applied for Benjamin, Dale was given a $1,000 raise.

One thing still bothered us. We did not have a baby sister for the boys, but with Vicki in Graceland and Susan attending a community college and preparing for a wedding, we really could not afford it. Then Dale was given another $1,000 raise.

As I was nearing forty, we decided it must be now or never so we applied for an all-Negro baby girl. We were told that girls were scarce and at my age it was doubtful if we would be able to get one. We left the matter in God's hands, feeling that He knew what was best for us. A couple of months later our caseworker called and told us he had a baby girl for us—perfectly healthy and all black. When we went to see her all she did was look at us and scream. She had blotches all over her body—an allergy reaction to penicillin given her for a cold—and she was definitely not happy. Despite her response we passed the test and the adoption was approved. When we brought her home a month later—at nine months of age—she cried and hid her head if anyone even looked at her. Now we have had Sarah for a year and she is a happy, outgoing, beautiful child.

We have encountered various reactions to our integrated family. Some people feel we are not being fair to our own children; some feel we are not being fair to our adopted ones. Some feel that the church and the world are not ready for total integration. We know that these youngsters will encounter problems, but we are trying to prepare them to deal with these. They will have to learn to live with criticism and nonacceptance in certain areas. Hopefully, society will change with the coming years. Dating? Marriage? We can only hope that they will ask their heavenly Father's help in finding solutions to these problems. In the meantime we shall love them and try to make them feel as secure as possible.

* * *

Not everyone has the motivation, the patience, or the financial resources to adopt children. All, however, can extend the hand of friendship and goodwill. Surely the simple act of "Getting to Know You" (as Rogers and Hammerstein put it) is still one of the best ways to break down racial prejudice. Jeri Auerback spearheaded a group in Texas with this goal.

* * *

Lillian looked so small, so fragile. I put my arm around her, and we stood close for a long moment sharing unspoken feelings. Her husband had been killed in an airplane accident. I'd been praying for her since I'd gotten word: "God, please bless her with your peace and grant her the strength she needs." As I walked to her front door I was praying, "God, help me as I visit Lillian to bring her comfort in some way." Whenever faced with the desire to comfort someone who has lost a loved one, I've always worried about what I should say. I didn't need to say anything to Lillian. The hug was enough. What it meant to her, I don't really know. I do know what it meant to me: a timber added to my own personal "bridge" to understanding.

Lillian and I are not close friends. We're more, perhaps, close acquaintances. Both of us belong to the same League of Women Voters unit, but we see each other only at meetings. In the past I would have been very conscious, going to Lillian's home, that I was white and she was black. I thank God that the prayer in my heart that day was totally concerned with bringing loving comfort at a time of great need. Yet the very sharing of this experience indicates that there is still a consciousness of "black and white." What gives me hope is that for a short time I wasn't aware of it.

As a white person I'm not sure we should become completely unaware of others' color because it's a part of their heritage, and I feel it's important to appreciate the culture and history of other races. I first felt this need for mutual appreciation several years ago—and wanted to help others feel it too—when I had the opportunity to present a proposed intercultural activity to our district women's meeting, basically suggesting the value of person-to-person contact between women of different cultures. Because we live in Texas, this applied especially to black and white women.

The proposal, which was adopted, suggested beginning with a study course relative to where race relations are now and how we arrived here, followed by the organization of a women's intercultural group. One of the women's departments did have such a study course, and another invited a People-to-People panel for a meeting. But no group was interested in anything more. I became very discouraged, since so much effort had gone into drawing up the proposal and planning an initial workshop. I had interviewed people by phone and in person gathering information that we could adapt for our needs. All along the way I had prayed for guidance and felt so "right" about the women of the church reaching out in this way in our community where good race relations needed so much to be established. In my disappointment I withdrew into a little shell to soothe my wounded pride and anger.

Then one day I awoke to the realization that there were other white women who shared my feelings, and we few could still have this essential person-to-person contact with black women that we desired. We knew we must create the opportunity because our life patterns actually kept us from meeting Negro women except in very casual ways which didn't allow for any real communication. In my earlier interviews I had talked with a number of encouraging people who were willing to share their experiences and suggestions. One thing we were strongly advised to do—and we felt it wise—was to contact black women who were in the same socioeconomic level we were. Because so often whites have a tendency to be patronizing or paternalistic in relationships with black people, we knew that it was important to start off any association with some obvious basis of equality.

One of the church women offered to help get organized, and we served as cochairmen. We visited two established discussion groups in the city and were able to obtain the names of black women in our area who might be interested in joining us. We set up our first meeting and sent out invitations to the black women and our church women who had indicated an interest.

We were on our way! We scheduled monthly meetings, discussed our purpose as a group, and set up our program for the first year. After a year of Friday evening meetings, we named our group the "Friday Forum." We like this name because it reflects our openness to new ideas and our informality rather than the cultural makeup of our members.

Our purpose remains the same: we are primarily interested in getting to know one another in an informal setting and in an ongoing relationship. We're not out to rock the boat. We're not making big waves. We have yet to make any perceivable impression on other church members. But what we have done is to achieve a better understanding of each other's situation, especially in community life. I have found, for instance, that I'm much more interested in the candidates for city council and the school board, as well as fair housing laws, school integration, and antidiscriminatory legislation.

We found that we couldn't meet regularly over a period of time and not be influenced by the experiences and feelings of our friends: the importance for their children as well as our own to have the best schools and learning tools available, the impatience they feel when their children's future is at stake, their discouragement at the results of an election. We have begun to "wear their shoes," and know where they pinch and where the soles are thin, and about how long before a new pair will be needed.

As a group we want to serve others in some way, and at each meeting we contribute to a "kitty." At Christmastime one year we purchased sports equipment for an inner-city youth center. Another year we filled twenty-five Christmas stockings with fruit, candy, and games for the center's kindergarten party. We've also gathered food and clothes for needy families. Over the past several years we have invited guest speakers to come and tell us about the "help agencies" they worked with so we could determine where and how we could give support. One of the agencies we heard about—Inner City Parish—has a storehouse of donated staple foods, used clothing, and furniture. We invited the director to come and tell us about his work and were tremendously impressed with his efforts and continual need of community support. We determined that this next year we will donate double what we have in the past and contribute it to Inner City Parish for assistance to a college student.

What I've learned in the past several years of developing intercultural friendships couldn't be experienced any other way. No matter how many books or articles I've read or how many speakers I've heard, nothing could make as much impact on my life as the actual person-to-person experience I've had with the women in Friday Forum. We've questioned, we've shared personal feelings and experiences, we've learned. We've had a great time getting to know each other.

We may not be rocking any boats or making any waves, but we are building bridges in our own lives—bridges to understanding.

In Oklahoma marriage between whites and Indians is widespread and accepted, but the marriage of a white and a Negro is still strongly disapproved. And, of course, new morality notwithstanding, pregnancy before marriage is frowned upon. Here is the story of what happened to a girl with both those strikes against her.

* * *

[30] Doris and Bill first met in her parents' home. An older sister had invited some young people home for games and music, and Bill was in the group. They met again on the campus of the Junior College in Miami when Doris' high school class went over there for Senior Day.

They had their first date that day when Bill bought her a hamburger. They didn't really begin going together until that summer when Doris got a job working at the college and found that Bill had taken a summer job there, too.

My granddaughter Betty had gone to college in Iowa and in November Doris wrote her a letter saying that her folks were upset because they had found out she was dating Bill and planned to marry him someday. Betty wrote back that since Doris was eighteen she should be able to marry whomever she loved. Being part Indian Betty did not think it was terrible for races to mingle. Doris' family might not have felt the way they did if Bill had been an Indian, but they could not accept the idea of their white daughter being in love with a black.

When Betty came home for Christmas break, she found that Doris' folks had put her in the mental hospital in Vinita.

She said she was still in love with Bill and they could not change her mind, so she must be mentally unbalanced! Betty was convinced that Doris was not crazy, but she knew that when the girl was released from the hospital she would have difficulty finding a place to live. I told Betty she could stay with me, because I also felt that she should be able to make up her own mind, and she certainly needed time to think things out for herself without family pressure.

Doris was kept at the hospital only ten days because she was not insane and thus not eligible to remain. When I learned that she was pregnant I was a bit upset, because I've always been rather straitlaced about that sort of thing. However I again said that I would take her if she needed a home.

Meanwhile Bill was in Tulsa for the Christmas break with his family. He had been home only two or three days when he got a letter from Doris saying that she was in the mental hospital. He told his mother (who was really his aunt but she had reared him) that he had to go back to Miami but he didn't say why. My daughter Mary contacted him at the college and brought him up-to-date on all that had happened. She told him she would like to be his friend, as Doris was already her friend. Bill's voice broke as he said he certainly needed a friend.

When the hospital released Doris her folks picked her up and told her they would put her in a home somewhere until the baby came. They said she would have to give the baby up for adoption and give Bill up, too. Doris would not agree to this; she wanted both the baby and Bill. So, instead of taking her home, her folks dropped her off at the college with only $2.75 in her purse. She had a check at home for some work she had done at the college, so she got some friends to take her out there to get it. She stayed around the college with friends, first in one dormitory and then another. She did not have enough money to enroll the next semester. Finally I got word to her that she could stay with me. In the meantime she had applied for welfare, and by the time she came to me on January 28 that was all arranged.

I did some praying about all this because I realized I was getting into a touchy situation. I had been disturbed about remarks made by my church friends about the Negro people, and I had prayed about that, too. I hoped that somehow God might use Doris and Bill and me to help break down this prejudice.

Doris appreciated having a place to stay and someone to talk to about her problems. Blessed with a brilliant mind, she had made good grades in high school and college. She liked to talk about social issues and was eager to search for solutions. She had never had an active church life, although her folks were members of a Protestant denomination and all of the children in her family had been baptized. Bill had much more of a church background than Doris. He had given her a little New Testament and marked certain passages that he thought might help her. She read it faithfully every night, but she said she did not know how to pray.

One night before bedtime I asked her if she would like me to pray for her. She consented, so I stood with my arm around her and offered a short prayer. When it was over she said, "Granny, I never have heard my mother pray, and my mother never in her life mentioned to me about the importance of chastity."

Another night she found the Lord's Prayer in her New Testament and called to me, "Granny, here is where Jesus tells us how to pray." We discussed the prayer he gave as an example, and I told her that people in all churches use this prayer at various times, but most people do not realize what they are praying for when they say, "Thy kingdom come, thy will be done on earth as it is in heaven." I said that in his kingdom there will be no prejudice, no hatred. Then I told her that in our church we believe someday there will be a people who will work to bring about such a kingdom. Her remark was, "Fantastic!"

In my church school class we were studying a book titled *Spiritual Health,* and once in a while I'd read her some comment about the problems of our times. I told her that the author was a friend of young people. One night when I came home from prayer service I noticed that she had been reading the book. Later she told me that she had discovered an amazing concept in the chapter on "Sex." "Granny," she said, "I did not realize it, but I hurt Bill when I gave in to him."

Doris had not been here many weeks when she asked if Bill could come down for a weekend. I had never met him, but my children and grandchildren had always entertained their friends in my home so I had thoroughly expected to have Bill visit us. (Incidentally, I have been criticized for allowing this since it gave them the chance to "go on living in sin." In their defense I would like to say that they did not live as man and wife in my house or later at church camp where they went as our guests.)

When Bill came Doris wanted everything to be just right—for example, the food he liked . . . served by candlelight. When the meal was nearly ready a fuse burned out and everything went dark. We had to light the candles to see to put in new fuses so I could finish making the gravy on the electric stove. Doris almost had her candlelight meal from necessity!

Time passed. Doris was expecting her baby about the middle of June. School was over, and Bill was through at junior college. They had discussed marriage but Bill could not see getting married until he was able to make a living. It was hard enough for black people to find adequate jobs, and he thought he would need those last two years of college before he could expect profitable employment.

Finally he decided to go to Kansas City to look for work. If he found a good job, he planned to finish his degree at a college there. Before leaving, however, he came to visit a few days. While he was here, the baby was born—on May 27. It was convenient for me to have him here, because he could take care of my elderly father while I went back and forth to the hospital.

Bill went to Kansas City on June 3, but his plans for work did not materialize. The only opening he could find was a part-time job in a filling station, so he came back in early July. He still could not see his way clear to marry Doris, but he did tell his Aunt Pauline about some of his problems. (He still did not tell his mother because she had a heart condition, and he was afraid of what the shock might do to her.)

Mary and I suggested that they both go to family camp as our guests. We realized that this would be a first for the church people as well as for Doris and Bill.

Mary had paved the way beforehand. She and her husband had gone to an adult retreat a month earlier and at the last service she had told the story of the couple staying with me. They had had wonderful experiences at the retreat and the understanding and concern of the people there who heard the story made us certain that they would welcome Doris and Bill and little Chineeah.

I prayed all week that they would find a solution to their problems. Each time I petitioned the Lord I enjoyed a calm, peaceful feeling. My prayers were answered.

Bill served as a lifeguard and worked with the young people. Doris went to the classes and helped in the nursery. Chineeah was the pet of the camp. Both Bill and Doris like to sing, so they participated in the choir. All in all they were deeply touched by the way they were accepted. Some of the ministers talked to Bill, and I was happy when he came home determined to get married regardless of the lack of degree and the assurance of a financially secure future. They would go on faith that God would bless their marriage and help them in the days ahead.

The wedding was set for August 19 at my home. Doris went to see her folks several times, but they continued to give her a bad time and usually she came back crying.

Doris and Bill came home from family camp on Saturday afternoon and made plans all weekend. Monday night he called his mother and told her where he had been the past week. Then—all in one breath—he told her that he was marrying a white girl and that they had a two-month-old daughter. She was shocked, but she lived through it. She invited all of us to dinner the next Sunday afternoon. At that time she told me privately that he had been wise not to tell her before, because she would have worried herself to death if she had known he was in the midst of such problems.

Bill's folks paid all the expenses of the wedding. Bill wanted my large living room arranged as a small chapel with a center aisle. My daughter came from Temple, Texas, and played the organ. One of my grandsons, a minister, had charge of the service and another sang two songs, "Whither Thou Goest" and "What Color Is God's Skin?" Several of the church members who had been at camp came from miles away, and a few came from my home congregation. I was disappointed that some of the people I have loved for many years could not find it in their hearts to give this marriage the blessing of their presence.

All of Bill's folks came from Tulsa, and a few members of Doris' family attended. Her mother called the afternoon of the wedding and said she would not be there. I had never met her, but I asked Doris if I could talk to her for a few minutes.

I asked her again to come if she possibly could because I thought she would regret it all her life if she didn't. At the last minute she came.

Doris and Bill now live in Claremore, Oklahoma, where he is enrolled in college. They attend church regularly, and Doris has been baptized. They still have problems, but I feel—as I have told them before—that if they keep God in their family circle they will make it and be happy.

* * *

Doris and Bill face a very special problem. Many of the good people who have been able to forgive them for having an illegitimate baby have not been able to forgive them for the fact that one of them is white and the other black. It must hurt not to be forgiven; but perhaps it is just as hurtful to those who find they cannot forgive.

Interracial marriage is a touchy subject because it is such an emotional one. Almost as emotional is the problem of integrated housing. When Emanuel and Alice Etuk came to Indiana State University they tried to find an apartment in privately owned buildings close enough to the university that Emanuel could walk to class. (The university-owned housing for married students was farther away.) Their story is a touching one.

"I am not a bad man." Emanuel and Alice sat on the davenport, their faces stricken with hurt and bewilderment. They were from Nigeria and had lived with church people while they were at Graceland College, so this was their first meeting with American race prejudice. "Why are people so frightened when I say we want to rent an apartment in their house? I am not big or fierce looking. I have no knife or club to hurt them. Why is it when I call on the telephone they say

'Yes, we still have the apartment for rent,' but when I get there and they see I am black they tell me the apartment is rented now?"

Poor Emanuel. Poor Alice. They finally rented an apartment in a dormitory for married people, but it was rather a long walk on blustery winter days for a man used to equatorial Africa.

* * *

Alta Minthorn Stephens has taken an active part in the struggle to provide fair housing for blacks.

God touched me by making me aware of the devastating indignities black people face when they attempt something which most white persons approach matter of factly—obtaining housing.

In 1968 as a public health nurse for the Los Angeles County Health Department I was attending an all-day conference on children. Included in the conference was a fifteen-minute address by the director of the Los Angeles Metropolitan Fair Housing Center. The theme of her talk was the calamitous and dehumanizing effects discriminatory housing practices have on the growth and development of black children.

Her righteous anger so moved me that I began working part-time as a volunteer for the agency she headed. In addition I took part in the organization of a local fair housing council. As a member of this volunteer group I began assisting blacks who were looking for housing in my neighborhood—the Hollywood-Wilshire area. I looked for available apartments and houses in the newspapers, referred black home seekers to "for rent" and "for sale" signs posted in yards in the area, accompanied many blacks house hunting, and on several occasions where overt discrimination had taken place, made confrontation visits to apartments and houses in order to either persuade the manager-landlord to comply with the laws and make the dwelling available or to build a case for a lawsuit.

The hostility and hatred that poured out on me scared me at first. The "nigger lover," "traitor to your own kind," "why do you want to rock the boat," and just subtle suspicious attitudes came at me from all directions—neighbors, family, friends. There were times when I privately wished I had not become involved. But the more black people who came into my experience and acquaintance, the more I identified with them. The raw injustice of their being treated as undesirables in their mere pursuit of a place to live began to gnaw at me. I saw that I could no longer be naïvely comfortable in my house when all these black people were having an appalling time trying to get a manager to show them an apartment just so they could see if they *liked* it.

Also I began to see that any Christianity I possessed should, because of Jesus, be applied to this injustice being done to blacks, many of whom were now my friends.

For about two years my association with the fair housing organizations in Los Angeles improved my knowledge of discriminatory practices, equal housing laws, assembling evidence for and filing of lawsuits, skills in combating discrimination, and organizing grass roots fair housing groups. And, of course, it also helped me to become acquainted with a lot of black people.

Since moving to Independence, Missouri, three years ago I have not been as diligent as I should be in responding to God's movement in my consciousness. Now a new dimension has been added to discrimination in housing—that of economic discrimination. "If the family makes less than $7,000 a year . . . If the house they want to build is subsidized by the government . . . If the family received financial aid from the state . . . we really don't want them in the neighborhood, no matter what color they are."

I want to respond more to God's touch. I want to help my own community face the facts of racial and economic discrimination in housing. I want to bring relief from the complete frustration and utter despair I have seen reflected in the faces of black and poor homeseekers. I want to express my love for God and my fellow people in a very specific human service—making good housing and honest housing a reality in my neighborhood and my community.

* * *

It is never easy to be a pioneer in any field. Pioneering in racial integration and true brotherhood is no exception. Realistic Christians don't expect an easy victory. We know that we must expect heartaches and frustration and perhaps even danger, but we also know that God's kingdom will be built on earth and all of God's children will have an equal right to live there, secure in the equality of his love.

CHAPTER EIGHT

Working from Weakness

[31] The pastor and I were working together in the church office when he left me for a moment to go upstairs to find a reference we needed. When he came back he was looking a little agitated.

"There's a man sprawled on the floor of the vestibule," he said. "I don't know what to do for him. He must be sick or drunk . . . or something."

We went up together, and one look told me all I needed to know. The man was dead drunk, and it took me quite awhile to make any sense out of his mumbled replies to my questions. He lived in the neighborhood and had wandered into the church thinking he was home. I worked with him until he sobered up enough to get on his feet with my help. Then I took him home.

When I returned to the church the pastor said, "I couldn't have done that. Thank God you were here to take over."

"I was down that road myself not so long ago," I reminded him. "I know what it's like, so I know what to say and do for a drunk."

I'm not proud of my past. I'm an alcoholic—but a sober one. I sank about as far as a man can go and come back up again. All those bad experiences are still there in my memory.

I'm not boasting about them, but I find I can use them now to help other people who need the same kind of help that I needed a few years ago.

* * *

We can learn to work from our weaknesses. Past mistakes, illness, handicaps . . . all can be used to help people who may have similar problems if we allow God to direct us.

Like Wendell, Mary and Byrnes are alcoholics. They work closely with, although not always through, Alcoholics Anonymous. Their telephone may ring at any hour of the day or night with a drunken mumble at the other end. They always go.

¹¹ "Sober alcoholics" are people who have had the disease of alcoholism arrested, generally through a spiritual awakening. Because of their sobriety they often want to assist other alcoholics. Usually they are alerted to a need by having the names of alcoholics given to them by concerned relatives or friends.

Sometimes a person will come by himself. Lew, a restaurant owner, used to come by our place of business and say, "I've got a friend in Hamilton who's an alcoholic. Someday I'm going to bring him in so you can talk to him." After this had happened several times we received a phone call one morning at six o'clock. "Can you come over right away? This is Lew. I'm in terrible shape. There isn't any alcoholic friend in Hamilton . . . it's me."

We went over and found that Lew had left his call for help until it was almost too late. He went into alcoholic convulsions, and we had to get him to the hospital quickly. Fortunately, he recovered. We continued to work with him, over a period of time. He spent his first sober Christmas in fifteen years in our home . . . and he remained sober the rest of his life.

Mike was a mechanic. His wife called us one night when he had been drinking and had dt's. Again we both went over (a drunk at this stage can be hard to handle). We stayed with him all night and for the next three days, taking turns being in the room with him. He was really in bad shape, and his delusions kept getting worse. At first he thought he was being attacked by bees . . . he kept grabbing a handful of his clothing which he would twist and squeeze to "kill the bee." At one point he tore off all his clothes. He crawled under his bed and went through the motions of repairing a car. For a while he thought he had been in a car accident and his wife and brother had been killed.

We had a doctor in several times to give him medication to calm him down, but nothing really seemed to work. We were about ready to put him in the hospital where he could be placed in a straitjacket so he couldn't hurt himself when he finally began to come out of it. He calmed down and soon went into a sound sleep.

Later when he woke up and seemed to be himself again we talked to him. He went with us to an A.A. meeting, but he decided that this was not for him. Instead he joined a church, began attending regularly, became a Sunday school teacher, and in general was so changed that later his boss came to us and said, "What has happened to Mike is a miracle. He's a different man." Where he had been tolerated in a menial job because he was not reliable, he was now put in charge of a branch repair shop. Another drunk had been salvaged from alcoholism.

Sometimes prayers are answered quickly and an alcoholic responds to help almost immediately as Mike and Lew did. Other times we may work and pray for an individual for years and he never stays on the wagon. Take Ken. The shortest time between his binges was three months and the longest was three years. We were thoroughly depressed when he called and said he was at it again. But we couldn't let that stop us. We just kept praying and encouraging and hoping that the next time he says, "I've had my last drink," he will mean it.

* * *

Work from weakness! A physical disease or handicap may lead a person into a form of service he might never have thought about if he had been physically healthy.

" I first met Kay Goldbeck at Camp Farthest Out. She had an incurable disease that was so bad she had to be carried up and down stairs. After the camp was over, friends began bringing her to our Thursday night study group, and her religious life deepened.

The Lord laid it on her heart to open a center for people to come to rest and be rejuvenated and healed. She began to look and found property in Orangeville that sounded right. We took her up there and found it was just not suitable. Then she heard of another place in the same general direction. Again we took her to see it and were appalled. Although it was run down and dilapidated, Kay agreed to take it. We couldn't see why, but she said she felt the Lord was leading her.

To clinch the deal she had to have $2000 for the down payment by December 24. She decided to make this a faith venture; none of us would tell anybody. The money must come in without our asking for it. It seemed evident that God was really behind us because Kay would call and report that she was getting checks in the mail and dollar bills, and people would come to see her and empty their pockets before they left. Many felt compelled to send her money without knowing why.

December 24 came and she had exactly half of what she needed, but she wasn't disturbed. My husband was to take her to the bank to deposit the money, and she was quite confident that the other thousand dollars would come in before the day was over.

Just after they left for the bank, our phone rang. It was a woman trying to find Kay. She said that for the past several days she had felt she should transfer $1000 from her bank account to Kay's and was trying to find her to complete the transaction. I ran out and stopped them just as they were turning out of the drive. Kay came back to the phone and arranged for the transaction. the woman phoned the bank, and the needed $1000 were in Kay's account before she even got there.

As I said the place was run down; there was no furnace in the house, and the grounds had been completely neglected. The first thing we had to do was pray for money to fix it up. Kay, still going on faith, moved in with only an old cookstove for heat. Since she was sick she couldn't do any of the work herself, but a friend wrote: "The Lord tells me you need me. Can I come up and help you?"

This woman stayed a year and was a tremendous help. She built a stone fireplace and converted what had been a woodshed into a comfortable lounge.

An old man who needed a place to live showed up one day. He stayed, too, and took over the carpentry work. He supervised construction of a bath, additional rooms, attic, dormitories, and a meeting hall. Somehow there were always people to help, and there was always money when it was needed. Now Singing Waters can accommodate seventy-five people at one time.

A retired teacher has built a cottage on the grounds and helps with the work.

A woman discharged from a mental hospital went to live there as a patient and stayed on to become the cook. She also helps guests with mental and emotional problems. In addition to this she earns money teaching music in the public schools and sings concerts in the area.

Several boys living in the neighborhood started dropping by to mow lawns and help with the garden and yard work. Some of them are now married men who still come back on their summer vacations to take care of the jobs that Kay and the other year-round residents can't do alone—wash windows, construct or repair buildings, and mend fences.

A fairly recent addition is the Chapel in the Woods. This is an outdoor chapel built at the back of the property where a river winds through the fields and woods. Incidentally, the beauty of this spot with the water trickling over the rocks inspired the name Singing Waters.

As the physical reality of Kay's dream, Singing Waters is a rehabilitation and retreat center for anyone who needs rest and spiritual uplift in an atmosphere of love and caring. Guests are referred in by people who know of this place and what it can do. There is no set fee charged. Guests give what they want to and can. Otherwise, Kay depends on donations coming in to defray expenses. Sometimes things get pretty meager, but when she is down to her last dollar, another check always comes in.

Over the years people with mental and emotional problems, alcoholics, unwed mothers, and delinquent minors have been helped. There was, for instance, the pregnant, incorrigible girl who through Kay's love, was able to find a new self and a new kind of life. Another fourteen-year-old girl was brought by her father . . . who left her and never came back. Kay reared her and sent her to college.

Kay herself seems physically healed of her "incurable" disease. Certainly she is in better health than she has been for many years. But she is getting older, and the years are beginning to take their toll of her energy, though her enthusiasm and loving concern are undiminished. Looking ahead, she is already praying for someone to come in and learn to run Singing Waters as it has always been run . . . for the benefit of people who need loving care.

* * *

Work from weakness! Mental and emotional problems can make a person not only more sensitive to similar needs in others but wiser and more patient in helping them.

[32] My father was obsessed by adoration of his mother. When she died and I was born, he transferred that obsession to me in the form of jealous possessiveness. I lived in fear of him, for I did not dare to displease him in the least way. I grew up in bewilderment and constant turmoil.

Ideally the love of God is taught to a child through his parents' example, but a child born into fear of parents who have not been taught divine love themselves does not have this blessing. After years of anguish, I discovered God's love which, at last, freed me to love and be loved. Because of my gratitude I promised that, weak as I was, I would try to help other troubled souls.

I soon discovered that service to such people meant learning how to love them when they were the most unlovable. I had to learn forgiveness even when there was no repentance on their part and seemingly no desire to change or help themselves. Ruth Ann was the product of three generations of disturbed people (from both sides of her family). She had spent eighteen of her thirty-six years in mental hospitals. The first time I met her I knew I could never help her alone. Without divine strength and wisdom there would be no hope for one so ill. Yet her need was so great and she would not agree to seek further professional help because of her fear of doctors and hospitals.

Ruth Ann had tried to support herself but she had failed to keep a job because she couldn't get along with people. Most of her problems seemed to stem from a deep feeling of terror and guilt. When I met her she had no money, no food. Her rent and utilities had been paid by the church. She had had so little experience in taking care of her own needs that she was quite inept at shopping and cooking. She would not readily accept help from me and got worse and worse until she had to be forcibly hospitalized by the authorities.

Since the hospital was overcrowded, Ruth Ann was dismissed much too soon. A friend and I took care of her, since she had no money and no relatives who could help. The church gave her money for food; I managed it and helped her do her shopping, acting as her guardian and friend. The only counsel I tried to give was direction to God. My hopes and prayers were that she might "break through" to God and live a healthy spiritual life.

Caring for her physical needs was not the major problem. She was often in a state of hysteria and needed to take medication, but she was so afraid of hospitals that to go there to get medicine would have done more harm than good. Her psychiatrist allowed me to pick up the drug and administer it. This worked out well for a while, but success was short-lived. The psychiatrist was replaced with a different doctor who would not cooperate in this way. Ruth Ann refused to go to the hospital or to the doctor's office, and the hysteria quickly got out of control. This time, however, it was not necessary to call the police for commitment for she trusted me enough to let me take her to the hospital. That in itself was a big step forward; previously she had trusted no one.

After a year of hospitalization, she has improved enough so that now she is able to live and manage her life fairly well in an apartment of her own. For the first time she is holding a job satisfactorily and feels needed. I really have hopes for Ruth Ann.

Then there is Barbs. I first heard about her four years ago. She had been referred to a psychologist in hopes that she might make a better adjustment to the special school she attended. She was a thirteen-year-old retarded epileptic. The burden of handicaps this child carried was nearly unbearable; in addition to this, she lived in a broken home with a mother who had to work, leaving the two girls to shift for themselves. The sister is also seriously disturbed, but it was Barbs who needed immediate care. Her life was actually in danger as the sister often attacked her. The constant teasing and harassment had caused Barbs to be rebellious and aggressive in her own way. Many people had tried to help but nothing short of taking her out of the environment and giving her constant love would be effective.

Her need kept bothering me and would not let me rest. Or rather I should say the Lord was giving me my next assignment and, like Jonah, I was trying to say "no" by making all kinds of excuses. Wherever I went I would hear about her trouble. It haunted me until finally I said, "All right, Lord, I'll take her and try to do my best for her, but you'll have to help me."

It worked wonderfully for a while, but after she had been living with me for about a year she became so unmanageable that there was nothing I could do but have her go back to her home.

One morning I was feeling particularly sad because I had failed. At the breakfast table I leafed through a copy of

Restoration Witness. When I laid it down I felt a strong urge to go back and get it, and I finally did. I opened it to an article by a pastor of a difficult congregation who had prayed about his problems because he felt he had failed in his ministry. The Lord told him, "You are called only to *assist* in the building of my kingdom."

I knew the Lord was saying the same to me, for since Barbs had been back home, many other people had been trying to help the whole family so that the mother and sister were also being benefitted. Barbs herself had become quieter, although she seemed to be regressing in other ways. It saddened me to see the whole year wasted, so I took her back. I am depending on the guidance of God's Spirit to help Barbs and, as in Ruth Ann's case, I have hopes for her now. I believe that, given a little more time and love, she can become the happy person the Lord created her to be.

* * *

Work from weakness! The heartbreak of parents who find a physical disability in their child can fester as a cancer of guilt and anger that destroys the child, or it can be converted into service that heals the child and reaches out to heal others with a similar disability.

[33] It seemed strange to us that our son Greg seldom responded to his name unless he was looking directly at us. He was a cheerful child who seemed to have an extra long attention span for an eighteen-month-old. Often he would play with his toys quietly, seemingly unaware of the other activities around him. Every now and then he'd look up and smile and jabber to whomever was nearby.

One day as I was ironing I recalled a movie in which a young couple discovered by accident that their baby was deaf. Greg was deeply engrossed in play near the couch with his back toward me. I called his name, and there was no response. I crept closer, calling him each time making my voice louder; still no response. Wanting to test further I took a pan and a wooden spoon from the kitchen and banged it loudly behind him. Nothing! I stood there quietly in disbelief. Than Greg turned his head and smiled brightly in my direction, but there seemed to be wonderment in his eyes—why was I standing there looking at him that way? I picked him up and hugged him as my mind focused on the realization that he could not hear me. Greg was deaf!

Later that day when Dale returned home from work and I relayed my discovery to him my emotions seemed under control. Somehow I felt a quiet reassurance that we would know what to do. I realize now that God already was blessing me with the strength that I would need to help my husband make his adjustments to our situation.

A visit to the doctor and audiologist confirmed that Greg's hearing was impaired. We were advised that little could be done until he was three and ready for preschool.

Every day in a young child's life is important, and I sensed—I'm sure through God's Spirit—that there were things I could do. From the John Tracy Clinic in Los Angeles I received suggestions for teaching Greg words and concepts necessary for everyday living.

Three weeks following Greg's third birthday, my husband approached me with strong feelings about asking for a special blessing for our son. After much preparation we met with the minister. The experience was filled with a beautiful spirit of reassurance. Although Greg was not healed, we were counseled to seek every avenue of education, science, and medicine and assured that our son would have a productive, rewarding life.

We have sought to follow this counsel. We have worked diligently with Greg, requiring speech in every event and action of life. The result, at this point, is a hearing-impaired child who can lipread and express himself in simple sentences.

The direction our lives have taken has been interesting. As we worked with Greg daily our interest grew keener—we wanted to know more about the hearing impaired. Observation rooms were available at the Preschool for the Deaf at K.U. Medical Center and I spent every moment I possibly could watching the teachers. God seemed to quicken my mind so I readily understood the techniques. Soon the teachers asked me to help in the classroom. Then one afternoon the supervisor called to see if I would consent to attend a conference at Olathe, Kansas, for parents of young children who had been diagnosed as hearing impaired. The purpose of the conference was to teach these parents how to work with their children. I was astounded at her request that I help teach these parents, for only graduate students had been given this responsibility previously She assured me that I was capable, saying I was a "natural teacher" in this area.

God had moved in my life, guiding my thinking and understanding so that I could serve in this way. Later the director of education in the graduate school mentioned to my husband that I would be a perfect teacher of the hearing impaired and that it was a shame my undergraduate work was not complete. While visiting with Dale, she inquired about his future plans, then offered him a scholarship in the graduate program for training teachers of the hearing impaired.

Dale has only four more hours left before obtaining his master's degree in deaf education. While working toward this goal he has taught the hearing impaired in the Kansas City School District and is presently associated with Consolidated School District No. 2, Raytown, Missouri, where he has implemented a program for the hearing impaired. The program is built on the oral education philosophy, which we feel prepares the hearing impaired more adequately to face life in a sound oriented world.

One way we have found to inform people about the hearing impaired is through our unique Christmas activities. For several years now we have been Mr. and Mrs. Santa Claus for individuals in their homes, groups, and organizations. Our goal is to earn money to help defray expenses of educaticnal equipment needed to teach people with hearing difficulties.

Our hope is that all of us will find how God can work through us to help others when we commit ourselves to his service and promise to let his will be our guide.

* * *

Work from weakness! Perhaps the most heartbreaking experience parents can have is to be told that their child is mentally retarded. James and Alyce Ball have been through this sorrow and have used it not only to strengthen their own family life but to reach out and help others.

"Your child is mentally retarded . . . a mongoloid."

The words came reluctantly from the doctor leaning on the table across the room as if he, too, needed support. Obviously, telling a mother her baby is retarded is one of the most difficult things a physician ever has to do.

I stood for a moment looking down at my beautiful baby. My first thought was, How can he tell? My legs were weak, but I stood holding my baby closely while my mind tried to take in the meaning of the doctor's words. What did "mongoloid" mean? He said that she would be slow, but there was no way of knowing how slow. He suggested I take her to another doctor. I agreed. I would not run from doctor to doctor but there was one very special doctor we must see . . . my cousin, Dr. Richard A. Guthrie. Although he lived in another state, I knew I would feel better if he would look at Susan.

When I returned home our older children, aged nine, seven, and three, met me with anxiety mirrored in their faces. What should I say to them? Instinctively I prayed, "If this little one has been given to me for a reason, please, dear Lord, open my eyes to this reason. Help me to know thy will, and I shall do my best to serve." I would tell them the truth, and together we would journey down this pathway. Each step would be discussed openly and honestly.

"Honestly," I said, "I know little about mongolism, but we'll find out. God has entrusted Susan to us, and we'll do the best we can." I knew that I must watch over Susan and give her all the love and special care she needed, but the other children must have a normal childhood—not one that revolved about a handicapped baby sister. We held hands and prayed that God would be with us and give us the help we needed.

We watched with deep concern every movement Susan made. During the next two years we celebrated many events: her turning over, her first smile, her first giggle. These accomplishments usually take two months in normal children, but for a retarded child they may take up to two years, and that is a long time for anticipation.

Loving Susan came easily, but not the disciplining. I decided that for her own sake as well as that of the other children I must discipline her as normally as possible. I soon found out that I had to be firmer with her, for once she decided to do something she was most determined. When I scolded her, her bottom lip would pop out and her head would go down or she would turn to her brother or sisters and run into their open arms. It was difficult to get the children to understand that Susan must be corrected. Turning away from those beautiful tear-filled eyes was not easy for them.

Susan was our doll. When she was three years old and weighed twenty pounds, she went off to school. As usual a first in her life was very important to the rest of the family. The children rushed home to see how she made it.

Susan enjoyed school, so for the first four years I drove sixty miles a day taking her back and forth. By receiving help at home she was ready to go into trainable school at the age of five and a half—a wonderful step forward.

Many people who have come in contact with Susan have been helped, encouraged, or enlightened by her winning smile and bubbling personality. High school and college students have written papers or given talks about her, and she has even gone to class with them. We have had the opportunity to show slides and give talks to PTAs, schools, churches, and hospitals.

Since Susan's birth many things have changed concerning the mentally handicapped. Terminology has changed too. The word mongoloid has been replaced with Downes Syndrome. We like to think we have played a small part in helping others to understand this affliction. One thing I have been especially interested in developing is material about Jesus that these children can understand.

I believe that Susan was given to me for a reason. It has opened many doors of service that I would never otherwise have discovered. People ask me how I can find the strength to serve in this way, and my answer is always that it comes from God. A day does not go by without prayer. I don't just kneel and pray; I talk to God as I wash dishes, clean the house, or work in the yard; I need him every moment. With prayer the family of a mentally handicapped child can have a very normal household. The lives of other children will not be marred if the love and care of a special child is made a cooperative family venture. Instead of being hurt by the presence of a mentally handicapped person in the family, normal children may grow up with a greater ability to love, a deeper understanding, and more compassion for others.

In trying to get as many people as possible informed about retardation I have found that the phase that interests me most is the traumatic moment when the parents are told that their child is retarded. I have written a pamphlet to help such parents. It is called "You Are Not Alone."[35]

* * *

Work from weakness. It isn't easy but with God's help it is possible. We must learn to accept a weakness. We may not be proud of it, but we don't have to be ashamed of it either. Instead, we can make our weakness work for God. Out of our weakness we may be able to perform a service that no one else can do.

CHAPTER NINE

"You're Never Too Young"

[34] It's a beautiful day; the sky is blue, and the sun is shining. I'm on my way to pick up Jean for church. As I stop the car, she hurries over, calling excitedly, "Guess what I got on my last lesson?" Before I can answer she bursts out, "Ninety percent—would you believe it?"

Can this bright, cheerful person be the same woman I first met two years ago? I had volunteered to teach crafts to mental patients in our local hospital when I came across Jean. She shuffled with the other patients—head down, dull eyes, straggly hair, and very much overweight. After I had explained the craft to the patients, most of them started on their projects; Jean, however, only sat—not wanting to do anything. I learned afterward that she had just attempted suicide. I tried to talk to her, but there was little response.

Our paths had crossed and somehow I couldn't forget her. Maybe I could show her someone cared and help her find her way back to a happier world. As the weeks passed I continued to visit Jean, and gradually she began to accept me as a friend. When she improved enough to be released she moved back home with her mother, but she was still depressed. Her future didn't look very hopeful; she had few friends, little training (except as a waitress), no goal. The turning point in her life came when I invited her to church with me. I had felt rather hesitant about it, wondering how our little group would react to her. And what would Jean think of a church that had only twenty members and met in a school? It soon became apparent that my fears were groundless. Our mission accepted her with open arms, and according to Jean the most valuable gift she's ever received was an introduction to Jesus. In him she had found faith in herself as a worthwhile person, hope for the future, and an assurance of God's continuing love. She passed milestones a few months ago when she began a course in home nursing and went on a diet (resulting in a thirty-pound loss). Jean's life has changed direction and hopefully will continue upward.

Allan sat beside the stone fireplace, strumming his guitar and singing. His foot kept time to the music and his face had a happy glow. The group around him listened attentively. Allan was at a camp for the mentally ill; he was finding happiness in giving of himself and in sensing the joy his music was bringing to others. It was several years ago that I first came across Allan when I took a group of patients bowling. He seemed eager to have someone listen to him, and he talked steadily about himself. I learned that he was an alcoholic and that his mental problems had begun when he was fourteen. Since that time he had been in and out of institutions. As Allan talked I realized how alone he felt; for him the world seemed a fearful place. Through various volunteer activities at the hospital I came to know Allan much better. He visited in our home and went on some outings with our church young people, even though he was much older than others in the group. When they had their programs at a nearby mental hospital he enjoyed using his musical talent. A highlight in Allan's life was attending a special camp for the mentally ill. He often talks about the wonderful time he had, sharing his music, playing crib with the patients, and most of all making new friends. Allan still faces many problems. He lives in a rooming house far from his family, is on welfare (as employers are reluctant to hire former mental patients), and has few friends in the area where he lives. He is often depressed, discouraged, and lonely, but I feel that because our paths have crossed, Allan's world is a little brighter.

Lorna came over for afternoon tea a few months ago and brought with her a book of stories and poetry which she had written. She proudly handed it to me to read. Lorna was an outpatient from the psychiatric ward when I first met her at a craft program. She, too, faced a lonely, hopeless world. Because the other members of her family were ashamed to associate with her she lived alone. She spent most of her days in bed, anxious for sleep to blot out the emptiness of her life. Lorna desperately needed a friend, and this was a way I could help. She eventually agreed to accompany our church young people when they presented programs at the mental hospital. It was there that she became aware of many others whose lives were even bleaker than her own, and she began to respond to their needs. By helping them she developed a feeling of self-worth. With our encouragement she decided to try her hand at writing—something she had always wanted to do. About a year ago she found employment at a rehabilitation center, and continues to write in her spare time. Lorna continues to gain confidence and now looks forward to each day. For her, life has taken on new meaning.

Jean, Allan, and Lorna are only a few of the people whose paths have crossed mine since I began working as a mental health volunteer. How did it all start? Ten years ago when I became a member of the church I began to see people in a different light. Before, I had valued my friends, family, and those around me, but only after my conversion did I develop a concern for all people and realize the worth of every individual. Out of this attitude grew the desire to be of service to others. My point of entry came several years later when our youth group decided to have a service project at the Raymond Mental Hospital, an institution for chronically disturbed older women. As leaders of the group, my husband and I became very involved.

On our first visit to the hospital we were met by a group of indifferent, apathetic women who responded very little to our efforts to be friendly. As we continued our programs we came to know these women better and to understand their loneliness and lack of hope. For many patients we were their only contact with the outside world; now we are their family! They feel sad whenever any of the young people go away to college and ask about them often, hoping they'll return for the holidays. There is no longer the lack of pride in personal appearance that used to be so evident. When we go for a visit they are dressed up in their best clothes and jewelry; they wear lipstick, and their hair is curled. We are greeted by sparkling eyes, smiling faces, hugs, and cheery greetings. As we leave the hospital we hear, "How soon can you come again?" and, "Hurry back!" When we drive away we see faces pressed to the windows and hands waving. It's hard to leave them. A few of my favorite people stand out.

There is Beatrice—pretty and tiny—who wonders why her father hasn't come for her; she's been waiting for four years. Does she know he never will? She beams under our approval, has a smile for everyone and a great capacity for love.

There's Annie—heavy, grey-haired, with laughing blue eyes, who wishes she could see her daughter whom she hasn't seen for many years. In spite of her sore legs she's always ready to take part in the activities.

There's Kume—a small, bright-eyed Japanese lady—who loves to grow things. Her efforts to teach us her language must be discouraging, but she only laughs at our attempts.

And there is Ione, an Indian woman with long black hair, who desperately wants to go home. She clings so tightly to our hands as we leave that it's hard to say good-bye.

Out of our service at Raymond Hospital has developed a summer camp for the mentally ill which is staffed primarily by the church young people. Two such camps have been held, and plans are underway for one this coming summer. In addition to our friends from Raymond we take a few outpatients. These camps are a tremendous experience for all of us. Here we deepen our friendships, and for one week out of the year these patients become individuals with rights, whose ideas are acknowledged and used and who, once again, are accepted.

Until I became actively involved I didn't realize the joy that comes when one tries to help others. No one should say he has nothing to give, for I've seen how a little bit of love and concern can change another's life to give it meaning and hope. These people whose paths have crossed mine have given me much. They have helped me to be more understanding and to see that everyone is of great worth. I've developed a greater appreciation of my blessings and our family has grown closer as we've worked together. I place great value on these new friends and, somehow, as we walk along together the world becomes a brighter place for all of us.

Lillian Millar and her husband, who are young adults themselves, together with members of their youth group are providing real ministry to the mentally ill. And they are not alone. Young people across the country, both as individuals and in groups, are reaching out in service to others in their communities.

Hundreds of girls in Canada and the United States donate thousands of hours a year doing volunteer work in hospitals as Candy Stripers. Hundreds of others, like Heather Forfar, spend many hours on their own initiative visiting in psychiatric and medical hospitals . . . talking to patients, feeding them, helping them with crafts.

* * *

David Phipps, a teen-ager with a mature sense of compassion and responsibility for others, voluntarily began to visit patients in a local hospital. He read to them, talked with them, and frequently prayed with them. When he was graduated from high school he established a unique "first." He was asked to give the baccalaureate address for his graduating class—the first time such an honor had been given to a student.

* * *

Young people during an annual youth camp at Centralia, Illinois, give a day of their camp to service in the community. After an Emmaus meal in the morning they go out to the local nursing home to wash windows, do yard work, and other things that need to be done. In the afternoon and evening they stay on to sing, share, and visit with the patients on a one-to-one basis.

One year they brought a group of inner-city children out to their camp—a guest for every camper. All activities were centered around the visitors as they shared beliefs, problems, and discovered their differences and similarities. By the time the day was over all felt that they were cherished members of a caring family.

* * *

[6] Young people of Pensacola, Florida, are pioneers in a new kind of camping in their area. They contacted the United Cerebral Palsy Center in their area and offered not only their church camp facilities but a full staff of volunteers for an outing for c.p. patients. Through bake sales and other money-making projects they raised $550 ... enough to finance a four-day session for thirteen children without any cost to the parents. Activities included story time, crafts,

nature study, swimming, and campfires. The camp also featured a parade with flag-trimmed hats for all participants and crepe paper decorations for crutches and wheelchairs.

Throughout the camp the Leaguers displayed amazing patience and understanding. This was due in part to their orientation. Several had done volunteer service at the Cerebral Palsy School in Pensacola; others attended a seminar in which they became acquainted with c.p. patients and their needs. Both staff members and campers felt that the project was a success and should be repeated annually.

In a letter of appreciation which appeared in the *Pensacola News Journal* one of the parents wrote: "In a time when the news so often presents teen-agers as dropouts, copouts, and addicts, these young people give us faith in the world of tomorrow. May they be the gauge by which their generation is measured."

* * *

Young church members of the Omaha-Council Bluffs area received an honor plaque from *Parents Magazine* for their "outstanding service to the community" in conducting a camp for handicapped teen-agers in the summer of 1971. They raised $165 through "slave auctions," carnivals, and suppers to finance the project which was held at the church campgrounds. Campers participated in the usual activities and received no special treatment, thus providing a challenge for them to live in a world which does not change to accommodate them (this was done at the suggestion of the Easter Seal Society).

* * *

Three years ago Michael White left the North Carolina Memorial Hospital and went home to die. Both of his kidneys

were failing, and his family had no money to pay for the expensive dialysis treatments which could keep him alive until a transplant donor could be found.

Then eight high school students—four white and four black—heard about his plight and determined to raise money to buy the machine. Since it and the treatments would cost over $6000 the task seemed almost impossible, but the teen-agers were determined not to let Michael die.

The hometown newspaper gave the project plenty of publicity and other groups and individuals began to work too. The local high school donated receipts from a concert. A church youth group gave up a planned trip and donated the $200 it had saved. A local firm gave the profits made on designated days to the fund. In a nearby town a group of young blacks earned $103 for a badly needed fire truck, and the town sent it to Michael's fund.

In less than six weeks almost three times the amount of money needed had been raised. As a result of these teen-agers' determination and work, the hospital received a kidney machine and a trained operator, Michael was kept alive by treatments until a donor was found, and the entire community benefitted by having this expensive piece of medical equipment for others to use when needed. In addition, blacks and whites found they could work together on a project that all felt was important.

* * *

Two newspaper carriers in Independence, Missouri, combined two services in one. While working on their Boy Scout Life rank badge, Ron and Steve Gwinn helped the ecology by collecting 6,600 pounds of newspapers for recycling. When they sold the papers they received $28.32.

That may not sound like much, but the boys put it to good use by contributing it to the education of hyperactive children. All the work they put in the project became worth it when they saw the special equipment their contribution was able to provide: 16 heavy cardboard "bricks," four safety signs, a number line, and a set of tactile letters.

The boys chose to donate their cash gift to this particular service because Ron was once hyperactive but outgrew the condition. He and his family know how important special education is for children with this problem.

* * *

[35] Members of a youth group in Independence, Missouri, sponsored a caravan to an Indian reservation in Macy, Nebraska, to present a vacation church school. This caravan of sixteen youth and six adults ministered to more than one hundred and fifty men, women, and children.

Attendance grew daily as the news of the school spread through the community. Indian tribal officers publically expressed a deep appreciation for the work of the young people in providing Indian children with a "creative-something to do" and further expressed their gratitude for the fact that their children had been taught "the Bible."

"I am convinced that this outreach to Indian children was more beneficial to future ministry by the church than a dozen 'preaching series' geared to adults," the professor of social science at the church college said.

* * *

It took one teen-age girl to start an ecology program in Brazil, Indiana. Teena Fabbri opened a collection center for newspapers and glass containers. She and one of her junior high teachers manned the center on weekends. The building was unheated but they kept to their station even on bitterly cold winter days.

* * *

Young people in a church school class earned money and saved it over a long period of time. Instead of financing a trip or buying something for their church, they used the money to purchase a van and donated it to Singing Waters, the nonprofit rehabilitation center operated by Kay Goldbeck. This was one of the unsolicited love gifts that make such faith projects possible.

* * *

[6] In the fall of 1970 the young people of Spokane, Washington, area transformed the lower auditorium of the Spokane Southside Church into "Agape Inn." The attractive decor and coffeehouse atmosphere appealed to those who attended (over one hundred on the opening night), and the congregation decided to make it a regular Saturday night activity during the school year. It has provided an excellent opportunity for young people to develop their talent in folk and hymn singing, instrumental music, poetry reading, and storytelling, and it has also proved to be a source of outreach. As part of the program, youth share the "good news" of having experienced Christ working in their lives and in the lives of other people. Many times prayers are offered for those with special needs.

* * *

[36] "Please, may I have a big buddy." This has been the substance of a number of telephone calls received from time to time by Michelle Carman, director of the New Generation program at Graceland College. The request is directed to college students who are offering to serve as buddies for youngsters in the Lamoni community and surrounding areas.

Designed to assist children in becoming involved in some of the broader aspects of the community and to permit some expansion of relationships, the program includes anyone in the three to fourteen age group. Some of the children have problems. Others may have only one parent or come from foster homes.

When the program was being planned leaders contacted the local schools and as many parents as possible. Later the plan was presented to various groups on campus. At that point students were asked to sign up as big buddies. Initially only fourteen college men volunteered. This created some problems since there were forty-nine little buddies. The only solution was to assign some of the college women as buddies for the boys. With few exceptions, this proved to be successful.

The program has had a very positive response from both foster and natural parents. Many have expressed appreciation for what it has contributed to their children.

Since the big buddies have been encouraged to develop individual programs with their little buddies, some interesting and lasting relationships have resulted. Little buddies are invited to attend plays, sports events, movies, and other activities. This is in addition to or parallel with group activities—gym and swim nights, basketball and softball games, a Christmas party, Olympic and Kite day, and weiner roasts.

The basic aim of this outreach program is to help children to be the best of whatever they can be. Certainly it disproves the oft-repeated claim that college students are intent on disrupting and destroying the educational system.

* * *

[6] The Older Youth Service Corps provides opportunity for people to help those who are in need. Workers serve for

either an eight-week period in the summer or a full year or longer in projects similar to those performed by Peace Corps or VISTA volunteers. Initiated in 1964 the program has attracted many post-high school adults to serve in the States, Canada, Mexico, and several countries outside of North America. The volunteers pay their own travel expenses, receiving only room and board from their hosts.

Volunteers first served in Alabama in 1964 with traditional congregational ministries—vacation church schools, home visiting, and youth groups. In recent years, however, the trend has been toward more experimental ministries . . . assisting local churches and community agencies, serving young people and families with great needs—especially those from inner-city areas. These activities include supervising sponsored community playgrounds, camping with handicapped or disadvantaged children, and assisting in various types of community centers.

An example of a community service project is the preschool for neighborhood children operated by the Service Corps group assigned to Skewen, South Wales. While the school is held in the church and is sponsored by the congregation, the program is not church oriented and there is no charge for attending.

* * *

Sheri Grice, now a college student, tells of her experience with the Service Corps.

After graduating from high school, I went to Graceland College for a week at Leadership Training Camp. Having qualified for my water safety instructor certificate, I set off for New Hampshire with a ten-member team of the Corps. There, in the foothills of the beautiful White Mountains, we worked for eight weeks. Isolated on a large farm-camp, we had charge of approximately sixty-five children from New York City. Through the trials and successes of that camp, we watched the children grow, develop, and relax in an atmosphere where love and individual concern showed them a part of life which many had never known before.

Not only did the children grow—we grew too. We grew to understand people whose way of life was completely foreign to ours. How often we take for granted our quiet, optimistic lives, knowing that our strength comes from God, not man, and that His kingdom is inevitable. We found that for many people hope is unknown, love is superficial, and God is only the prefix to a four-letter expletive.

We who had caught a vision of something better knew that we had to share it. In my three years at Graceland I have seen the Spirit move many young people to serve in areas of need. It is my hope that their numbers will continue to grow.

* * *

Children of the junior church age (ten and under) of an Indianapolis congregation made flowerpot arrangements of plastic flowers at Easter. When the women of the church served their regular monthly dinner for the senior citizens, the children placed their flowers at each place. Admittedly some of these were a bit odd-looking but there were no art critics at the dinner. The senior citizens felt that every flower arrangement was beautiful. Both young and the old found joy in this project.

* * *

Richard and Ellen, two older teen-agers of Simcoe, Ontario, share their experience with senior citizens:

For the past year we have been visiting the Norview Home for the Aged where many beautiful people live because some disability prevents them from staying in their own homes. Our first meeting with them came about in early June 1972. As we sang and had fellowship with them as a group, we knew there was a need here that we could fulfill. The following Sunday we decided we must go back to Norview.

We thought one thing the residents would appreciate most would be outings. For the first couple of months we had no set pattern as to the number of residents we took out or where. Then, in the latter part of August, the administrator of the home suggested that we choose two of the residents to work with from then on. The reason for this, as he explained, was that these people had very little to look forward to, and once we had started to take them out each one expected to go every time.

Months passed, and we got to know the residents better as individuals with distinctive needs and desires. By taking them to picnics, hymn sings, church activities, and social events in the community we felt that we were helping them to better adjust to life at Norview. To further fulfill their personal needs we took them to visit their friends. We had a birthday party for each of them in the home of a friend.

The residents we have been taking out have become very attached to us—and we to them. Many have received Christ in their lives; this has made them more receptive to the love we offer them and they, in turn, are able to give it to others in the home.

There is a great need in places like Norview for volunteers who are willing to give of themselves and their time to help people renew the spark of hope they need to carry them on from day to day. Many such residents feel that once they are placed in a home for the aged their lives are over. What most of them need is someone who cares and is willing to give them the friendship, love, and companionship they desire.

Other young people are finding that in large group efforts they can serve whole communities:

[6] In a district which encompasses over six thousand square miles a special effort is required for young people to organize any kind of unified program . . . but it *can* be done. In February the youth of Central Washington District met at Moses Lake and voted to combine their talents in the production of "Jesus Christ and Company." The first performance was at a conference in March; after that there was at least one presentation a month. The cast of over sixty from various parts of the district had to practice in small groups until the day of the performance; then a complete rehearsal was held immediately before the presentation.

The group is not limited to church members (at least fourteen in the cast are not). For all, however, the project has been a faith-building experience. And this goes for the audience, too. Both performers and listeners have testified that "J.C. and Co." has changed their lives. One of the most rewarding presentations was for the inmates of the penitentiary at Walla Walla, Washington.

For some of the cast this undertaking has meant traveling over two hundred miles and giving up sports events or taking time off from work in order to participate, but the rewards have been worth it. The goal of the performers is to bring people closer to God, and they feel that this mission is being accomplished.

* * *

Young people of imagination and energy are finding plenty to do in varied fields of service. They are proving that they really believe what they read in I John 3:18: "Love must not be a matter of words or talk; it must be genuine and show itself in action."

CHAPTER TEN

"...Nor Too Old"

[37] After sixty-five I did not anticipate any challenges. I expected everything to end when I ceased to be educational director at the School of Nursing—no classes to teach, no students to counsel, and no faculty to cooperate with to plan the curriculum and write accreditation reports.

My whole life since the summer of 1935 had been wrapped up in the School of Nursing, its students, and the hospital. My professional life was to end on May 31, 1971. I had had numerous sleepless nights worrying about what I could do after retirement.

Then came the announcement that a mental health center was to open in the "old nurses' home" on June 1, 1971. "Ah," I said, "here's an opportunity!" For years I had been interested in the field of mental health.

In 1946 I spent two months in a hospital for nervous and mental diseases as a patient. After that I became even more interested in teaching psychology and in preparing students for their psychiatric affiliative experience away from the home school.

Then came the first Friday in June, 1971, when all those who had signed up as volunteers at the Independence Mental Health Center met for instructions. On the following Wednesday two others and I were assigned to work at the Center all day. We were to answer the telephone, make appointments to see the psychiatrist, and answer the questions of visitors. We practically had a private line in to the Western Missouri Mental Health Center and made full use of it as we sought answers to our questions about procedure, policy, etc.

On that first Wednesday my boss (coordinator of the Satellite Clinics at Western Missouri Mental Health Center) called me into the office to talk privately. He said that I had been chosen to do this because of my experience in teaching in the school of nursing.

That afternoon we toured the Day Center at W.M.M.H.C. where I met the nurse coordinator and many of the therapists. It was all so new to me that I had difficulty imagining myself involved in such an undertaking. While there we visited the library, and I borrowed two books on psychiatric day centers so that I might familiarize myself with them. I put in two busy weeks reading and outlining these books.

In the meantime we started an afternoon's class a week with an occupational therapist. Here we learned how to relate to certain types of patients having a variety of psychiatric symptoms. We learned how to play games and do handcrafts. We also studied "awareness therapy," a form of group psychotherapy.

We decided to open the Day Activity Center on July 8, 1971. The director and I carefully planned the activities for that first day. We revised and re-revised it. Then the day arrived—but no patients did. We were disappointed, but we used the afternoon to practice various activities.

The following Thursday a patient came—one patient and five volunteers! The day was a success, due largely to the perseverance of that lone patient.

By the time D.A.C. was two years old more than seventy members had enrolled. Our responsibility has been to help resocialize these people so that they can take their place in society and function on a better level. We try to help them plan a future in the community making use of its facilities. A few who have not progressed have become inpatients at W.M.M.H.C. or State Hospital No. 2 at St. Joseph, Missouri. We try to accept these failures philosophically and work even harder to meet the needs of other members.

One of our earlier patients was a man in his mid-twenties who had very little to say. If our project was to write he always ended up with a blank paper. Only occasionally would he express himself verbally. In any type of artwork he usually drew a single narrow line of some pale color. One day he told us of seeing dismembered bodies lying around. We checked on his medication and found that he had lessened his dosage without consulting the psychiatrist. When we persuaded him to increase his medication he improved. He loved to play croquet, and I think if he had had the chance he would have played hour after hour every time the D.A.C. met. Gradually he grew well enough to learn a new trade with the help of the Missouri Vocational Rehabilitation and a Kansas City agency. Eventually he left home for the first time in his life and became a contributing member of society. He was one of our first successes. There have been many since.

It is a pleasure to see the change in people who come in shy, unsure of themselves, withdrawn, and unable to talk to the person next to them. They do a variety of handcrafts, making simple but pretty or useful things. They learn to communicate. They begin to straighten up to their full height. They look other people in the eye. They smile. They become more animated when they play games. Gradually they learn to enjoy participating in group discussions. They begin to express themselves more creatively in art, writing, and drama. They have *fun!* When at last they understand something about emotional health and how to promote it, they are ready to be on their own.

It is a glorious feeling to have participated in the

reclamation of one of these patients. Not only do they improve under the day activity program, but we—the volunteers—also profit. Often we feel that we get more than we give.

There are other volunteer tasks at the Mental Health Center—for example, receptionist (to answer telephone calls; make appointments for psychiatrists, psychologists, nurses, social workers; see that charts are ready for use and filed properly). At present we are trying to start a small library so that good material in the field of mental health will be available. There are supplies to be purchased for handcrafts. There is such a wide variety of work that no one becomes bored.

I am very happy that I was selected to help such a worthwhile cause.

* * *

We're never too old!

We're never too old to learn . . . to help someone else . . . to find new worlds to conquer. Many older people, like Vida Butterworth, are fortunate enough to find an area of service related to their vocation before retirement. Others must look for new interests to provide an outlet for their energy and talent.

Experts on the aging process have found that for a senior citizen to retire to a "well-earned rest" is the same as signing his own death warrant. With nothing to occupy his mind and energy, he simply waits for death—and it soon obliges. Keeping busy is the best way to assure a long and happy retirement.

Of course, people of other age groups can help by not shunting the elderly aside as though they were useless. One congregation has found that the best and most reliable official greeters at the door on Sunday morning are the senior citizens. Even those who are crippled and can no longer perform more active services can still minister with a friendly smile, a handclasp, and sincere words of welcome.

An example of one who has found a unique service is Grandma Mack of Minneapolis. An elderly woman whose ministry is prayer spends four . . . five . . . six hours a day praying—sometimes for people she knows, sometimes for people she has never met but whose names and problems have been related to her. "If you're on her prayer list," says Peter Gilchrist, "things happen!"

Many senior citizens find an outlet for their energy and love by becoming foster grandparents. For instance, in the Vigo County area sixty foster grandparents are working at different sites. They are assigned to such places as the Children's Learning Center; the Sheltered Workshop, where they help teach such skills as sewing; the local hospitals, where they visit the children's wards and cuddle young patients or play games to make the days seem shorter; the Happiness Day Camp, where they help supervise the playground; the Gibault School for Delinquent Boys and the Glenn Home for Orphans where they give love and companionship to youngsters who have had too little of both. To qualify as foster grandparents they must attend classes in a training program. The latest graduates run the gamut of races and include members of many churches from Protestant laymen to Roman Catholic sisters.

An elderly couple on an Ontario farm have found joy helping a young family:

[38] For the last ten years we have enjoyed the close association of a couple and their eight children. This began when we hired the father to work for us on our dairy farm and the family moved into a house on our property. As they

had no one else to turn to for help, our relationship soon became like that of parents and grandparents. Through illnesses, deaths, and financial problems we have been able to help and advise them.

The four girls and frequently the two little boys and another very small girl, all quiet and appreciative, attended Sunday school and church with us, filling a front pew and giving inspiration and joy to others. The oldest boy attended classes and with his mother joined the church. Later the rest of the family were dedicated to the Lord; this marked one of the happiest days of our lives.

When we sold our farm and retired we were able to buy and remodel a home for the family and help the father find a job. When this temporary employment ended they were unable to meet their normal financial obligations, so payments to us are being postponed or canceled.

The courage of these parents in their efforts to rear their children to be honest, hard-working, and respectful people in spite of their many setbacks is an inspiration to all of us and a witness to Christ.

* * *

Walter Cargyle is an unusually energetic and innovative senior citizen of Independence, Missouri.

[39] At an age when most people are thinking about relaxing ways to spend their retirement, seventy-nine-year-old Walter Cargyle is creating new organizations to serve his special interest group: senior citizens.

Walter began his volunteer work for senior citizens about twelve years ago when he was asked to head a newly organized club for the elderly people of his community.

During his first two years as president, the organization grew from 85 to over 400 members. It is still very much a going concern.

Walter served as president for seven years and during that time was named Western States Representative to the National Council of Senior Citizens as an organizer of senior citizen clubs in Missouri, Kansas, Nebraska, Iowa, and Colorado. In this post he organized approximately forty clubs, in addition to taking 150 members of his local group to Washington, D.C., for the national Senior Citizens Convention of 1964. He is still active in proposing and pushing plans for improving the lot of older people.

When he resigned as president of the Independence club he began looking for new projects and came up with the idea of a luncheon program for elderly and low-income people. He sensed a real need for an inexpensive program to provide well-balanced meals and fellowship.

The Stone Church, where Walter's club meets, offered the use of its kitchen and dining room facilities. Some food commodities were obtained through Human Resources Corporation; volunteers supplied the labor; and individual donations covered additional expenses. From serving 35 meals at the beginning, the program has expanded to an average of 150 meals each week, half of which are delivered to the handicapped and shut-ins.

"We're trying to put more emphasis on sending meals to those who can't come to us," Walter says. "Their need is usually the greatest. Often people living alone hardly know what a well-balanced meal is like."

After three years of operation this program received much attention as an avenue of service.

Walter helped get the program on its feet and continues to administer it. Now he has moved on to still another project—a senior citizen crafts store.

"I noticed so many seniors could make things with their hands but couldn't find ways of selling their wares. I thought it might be possible to start a retail outlet for their goods . . . a store they could manage for themselves."

More than 500 senior citizens merchandise their hand-crafted items at the store in the old Jackson County courthouse. A wide selection of ceramics, needlecraft, knitting, and other items are offered by the senior citizens who operate the shop. Participation is limited to Missouri residents who are fifty-five and older. About fifteen volunteers from senior citizens clubs of Independence and two part-time employees receiving state funds man the store during business hours. In 1972 the shop grossed $18,000. Ninety percent of the income from the sale of goods is returned to the person who made the merchandise.

Continuing as manager of the store, Walter has moved on to other efforts. Currently he is making arrangements for senior citizens to attend church camps.

Jogging may be next on his agenda. "I hope to start a Past Fifty Jogging Club within the next year," he says. "We'd have to start by teaching people how to walk right, then do stooping and bending exercises. I think there will be a lot of interest in this kind of program."

A retired physical therapist, Walter continues the practice of daily walking and has had experience in coordinating exercise programs at the Jackson County Hospital and senior citizens clubs.

"Everywhere I've been I've found that activity is the best way to combat the depression that often comes with old age."

When he reaches the age of eighty next year, Walter plans to cut back on part of his involvement in leadership activities. "I really don't ever plan to retire," he insists, "but I want to make the proper adjustments for a person of my age."

Old? Ridiculous! Walter Cargyle is one of the youngest persons in his community.

* * *

Jacqueline Flowers has written this tribute to an elderly friend who continues to carry on a lifetime tradition of active service.

My friend Dona is ninety-three now and lives in a nursing home. The nurses say they should be paying her to live there . . . she is so helpful with the other residents. She even visits shut-ins in the neighborhood on nice days.

She took me on the grand tour of the home when I last went to see her. Showing me the chapel she said, "This is where I come to pray for you, dear. . . ." In the employees' lounge a new cook asked, "Tell me again, please, what days you fast." In the therapy room—where people were producing ceramics, paintings, rugs, etc.—she said that she had tried everything and liked making hooked rugs best. Every one she had made had been sold in the gift shop. Dona says everyone needs something to look forward to, and she encourages all new residents to learn a hobby. She's blind in one eye but does not indulge in self-pity . . . rather she thanks God that she can still see out of the other one.

It has been a privilege to know her. I was her neighbor, and she taught me the meaning of stewardship, fasting, and prayer. Since I did not come from a church home, she "planted the seed" by taking me with her to prayer meetings. She demonstrated what she meant by stewardship by caring for preschoolers every day for years without pay. It was her gift to the mothers of our town.

* * *

Marian Ohmer tells of another senior citizen who refuses to consider herself too old to serve.

Margaret was sixty-nine when her husband died—an age at which many women would have "retired."

She stayed alone on the farm for a year, but when an opportunity came to live with a family and care for their baby girl, she took it. This one and the next baby of the family received her love and care until the mother quit work permanently.

Next, she stayed with an elderly woman for two years, doing her housework and cooking until the woman's health failed and nursing home care was required. A year's stay with an older couple, doing similar work, followed.

Then she bought a house close to the downtown area of her small town. In the large garden area adjoining her home Margaret raises vegetables, giving them to neighbors and family. The surplus she cans—to use herself and give away. Her flowers provide a touch of beauty in the neighborhood; these she shares with others and provides bouquets for the church.

When a neighbor needed a few hours' household help each day to enable her to work full time, Margaret offered her services. She made cookies, pies, and rolls for the family as well as straightening up the house and doing the cleaning. She continues to do this because she enjoys the family and wants to remain useful.

When the church needs pies, potato salad, or baked beans for its fund-raising dinners or food stand at the country fair, Margaret can always be counted on. In addition to this she supports the congregation with her attendance, financial support, work, and testimonies.

And Margaret does not have perfect health. Despite her ailments she gives thanks to her heavenly Father for strength in time of illness and bereavement—and for the joy she has experienced during her many happy hours.

Here, indeed, is a remarkable woman of eighty-three. She will be greatly missed when she passes on to her reward.

* * *

Many older people could shame those who are much younger by the extent of their activities as they continue to lead lives of service. Too old? They would stoutly deny it. People who care are never too old.

CHAPTER ELEVEN

"The Best That You Have"

[40] Tragedy can strike like lightning out of the blue, giving no time to prepare for it. It was that way for my neighbor on a summer day in 1972 when her son was touched by high voltage wires. Much of his body was severely burned. The doctors held out little hope that he would live overnight.

I rushed next door to take over while the parents followed the ambulance to the hospital. Later I joined them there to give what comfort I could by my presence and my prayers. Somehow, in that anguish-filled night, God let me feel the very emotions that my friend was feeling. It was as if my own son were lying there, and I was praying that he would live.

Garland clung to life, but his condition did not improve. He was in deep shock, and his physical resources were so far depleted that it seemed impossible to hope for his recovery. I longed to do something for his parents . . . beyond offering my love and prayers. The next morning I hesitantly offered them the very best that I have . . . my faith in the healing power of God through administration to the sick.

"Would you let me call the elders of my church to administer to Garland? My church uses this ordinance as James describes it in verse 14 of Chapter 5," I explained. "I want so much to give you the best that I have, and this is the best."

They were still too numbed to really understand what I was suggesting. Several days passed and Garland was still alive. There was no improvement; if anything, the doctors thought his condition was deteriorating. Two weeks after the accident Garland was rushed to the operating room for emergency surgery. While we waited for the outcome I felt an overwhelming compulsion to explain more about my church's belief in administration to the sick. I picked up a Gideon Bible to read James 5:14 to them: "Is any sick among you? Let him call for the elders of the church; and let them pray over him, anointing him with oil in the name of the Lord."

This time they understood and asked me to call the elders. The ministers came immediately, but they felt strongly that Garland himself should be conscious and aware of what was happening to him, so they waited until he came out of the anesthetic.

When they went into his room they told him of God's healing power through this ordinance and urged him to exercise his own faith as they placed their hands on his head. Both felt the strong presence of God and a deep assurance that Garland would live. He took a turn for the better almost immediately. The doctors began to issue more optimistic reports to his parents—cautiously at first, and then with increasing confidence. Where they had been putting off further surgery because they felt it would be useless, they now scheduled it and held out the first real hope that he would recover.

Two weeks later he had recovered to the point that he was able to walk a few steps. A year later he had completely recovered. We are still next-door neighbors, still the best of friends, and she still thanks me for my prayers and for bringing the elders to administer to her son. No, she hasn't been converted to my church, but she is more active in her own, and I know she feels closer to God than she ever has in her life.

Previous chapters in this book have contained examples of tangible service. Many people—like Ruby Sims—have found a new dimension in serving, and the results can be just as real.

Prayer for others is a service. Testifying of God's love and concern is a service. Telling the good news of Christ and his kingdom is a service. Physical bodies can be healed, minds and relationships can be improved, lives can be changed, the whole world can be made new by people who know God intimately and share their knowledge of him with others.

Small prayer groups have sprung up in many congregations, and lives are being changed because of them. The members of one such group in Indianapolis never pray for themselves or their own family. Their prayers are always for others.

Another small group started because several women at a coffee klatch felt moved to pray for each other. Barriers tumbled, and they found themselves sharing problems that previously had seemed almost unbearable. One woman said, "I had been feeling so depressed for such a long time I thought I couldn't carry the burden alone any longer . . . and now I don't have to."

A mother told of her teen-age son who suddenly stopped going to church. His friends and his life-style changed completely from the Christian influence of his home. Every night his mother kept a prayer vigil for all members of her family, particularly for this son. For five years he did not set foot in a church, bow his head when grace was asked at mealtime, or show any interest in God. Then suddenly one day for no reason he stopped seeing the friends he had been spending his time with, broke off with the girl he had been dating, and made a complete about-face. He became thoughtful where he had been completely self-centered, began going to church, and was ordained a deacon in his congregation. He was so completely different that his family could hardly believe it. It was as if God had suddenly reached him.

How? Through his mother's prayers? Why not? We can't pretend to understand *how* prayer works. We only know *that* it works.

* * *

Christian Ashrams feature prayer vigils that last the length of the conferences. These vigils begin at nine o'clock on Friday evening and end Monday morning at ten. A prayer room is arranged with Bibles, a notebook, and pens; someone is there day and night for the entire time. People may sign up for an hour or half an hour as many times as they wish during the weekend. Participants often testify that they have never felt so humble or so alive or so filled with the Spirit as during these vigils.

* * *

John Crabb is a great believer in prayer.

We were visiting Sam one night when his younger brother phoned and asked Sam to pray for him. Sam was surprised because this was the first time this had happened and he didn't quite know what to do.

I knew something about Danny's problems from what Sam had told me. This seventeen-year-old kid was strung out on drugs and in pretty bad shape. He must have been in really bad shape that night to call and ask Sam to pray for him.

Something came over me and I felt impelled to suggest that Sam call Danny back and ask if he would like to be administered to. After all, drug addiction is a sickness, and the things that lead to drug addiction might be called sickness too. I didn't say anything, but twice more this feeling came over me. Now, when the Lord tells me three times to do something, I don't fool around . . . I do it!

So I said, "Call Danny and see if he would like administration." Sam shook his head at first, but finally he made the call and all the time he was dialing I was praying, "Help Danny say yes." Sam was surprised when Danny agreed, but I wasn't. I knew the Lord was working with him.

We went over to Sam's parents' home and Danny was there. Sam, his father, and I are all lay ministers. Sam offered prayer; his father anointed Danny's head with oil; and then his father and I put our hands on Danny's head. I prayed and I heard my voice promising Danny that he would be freed of his addiction—but there was a responsibility laid on him too. Danny was to go back and tell his friends who were still on drugs about what God had done for him.

As far as I know Danny is still off drugs. It's going to be rough on him going back to his old associates and their hangouts to tell them about God, but I believe he'll do it. I'm praying he'll hang in there.

* * *

Sometimes the greatest spiritual service lies in the love and concern that reaches out to the hearts and needs of others.

A college student working in the summer and beset with problems wrote of her depressed mood to a friend. The friend answered immediately: "Something's wrong. Won't you tell me what it is? I may not be able to do anything about it, but at least you know I care." These were simple words, but they must have meant a lot to the student because even now—almost thirty years later—she still remembers them.

* * *

Dr. Roy Cheville, now retired from the faculty of Graceland College, had and still has the unique talent of making even the most casual visitor feel important. One of his students writes: "It didn't matter who you were, the minute you walked in he'd look up with that thousand-watt Cheville smile. He was always busy with papers to grade and lectures to prepare and books to write, but he was never too busy to see anybody. He'd push everything aside as though it didn't matter at all and the only important thing on his mind was 'you.' He really cared. He made you feel you were the most important person in the world to him right at that moment. A lot of people remember him because of his books or sermons or classes or campfire songfests, but I remember him because he cared about me as a person."

* * *

This is the testimony of Warren, now a lay minister, who was reclaimed from a life of secular pleasure through the efforts of Christian friends.

When I was in my late teens I stopped going to church and did just what I wanted. I joined the service and smoked and drank and gambled and played around with the worst of them. Then when I came back to Indianapolis and got with church people again, I didn't know whether I liked it or not. I still hadn't had enough of going my own way. But Johnny Crabb and the rest wouldn't let me go. I'd keep drifting away and they'd haul me back. I don't know why they kept coming after me—I certainly didn't help much—but they did, and here I am. I have God and the church and a fine family. Who could ask for anything more?

* * *

Here is a story from the other side of the fence. Greg Savage and several other church people in Holland cared enough to give of themselves to help some young men find God.

During the 1972 Easter Holiday when I attended the Dutch family camp I became aware of some problems among the young people. I mentioned my concern to a couple of others, and we talked for several hours about the problem, but no solutions came. We only knew that there was a tremendous amount of potential talent going to waste. Then we turned to our heavenly Father and presented our concern to him.

At a prayer meeting we were inspired to help bear their burden by praying for them and loving them as Christ did.

At that time I didn't know any of these young people very well, but it didn't take long to find an excuse to visit their congregation. Since they lived in North Holland and I lived and worked in Hannover, Germany, there was the problem of transportation. However, by planning ahead I was able to meet with them several times.

During the summer the first European Witnessing Weekend teams came from America. Their sacrifice and desire to bear testimony of Christ had a tremendous impact on these young people. Then came the International Youth Camp at Dunfield, England, in which over 700 campers from seven countries participated. They used three major languages in communicating the love of Christ to one another. However, when a special testimony service was held the Spirit of God was so powerful that language was not necessary. Brotherly love was expressed in the eyes and through handshakes.

One young Hollander I was concerned about was sitting on a bench in front of Dunfield House sobbing. He was experiencing the love of Christ so strongly that he couldn't hold back the tears. I put my arm around his shoulders, and asked him to take a walk with me. As we went down the driveway, two other young men joined us. We walked in silence until we came to a secluded spot. During the next forty-five minutes or so I talked to them about the experience they were having and their responsibility to God, to others, and to themselves. God used me to give them guidance and counsel. He put thoughts in my mind and words in my mouth. I was speaking English to them—which for them was a second language—and the Lord blessed them with understanding.

In September I received letters from two young men. Each expressed concern at not having the courage to stand and bear testimony or pray aloud in a group. I wrote and assured them that we would seek the answer together at their Mission Conference in October. I made their problem a matter of prayer, and days before the conference I felt confident that I had been given the solution.

After the opening activities, eight of us met to discuss how we could be better witnesses. We started with a prayer, asking for guidance. Once again these young men stated their concern. When all had finished speaking, I outlined a way in which we could support each other.

The next morning we sat together in the fellowship service. At a convenient time we all stood together, and each of us offered a prayer. For most of these young Hollanders, it was the first time to pray aloud in a group. Today all are active in their respective youth groups and choirs. They, too, are now seeking ways to bring others to Christ.

These young men have allowed Christ to enter their lives, and they have changed. This doesn't mean that they don't have any problems . . . they do . . . but they are assured of the blessings of God as they seek to do his will.

Because several of us took an active interest in these young people, the Spirit has been able to minister to them through us. Yes, the worth of individuals is great in the sight of God, and he uses those who are willing to listen and follow his direction.

* * *

Sometimes all it takes is someone to listen, someone to talk to, someone who cares. Someone like Wana McDole Taylor:

The barefoot, bearded young man beside me in line at the American Express office in Amsterdam was waiting to cash a check too. This busy office was a mecca for foreign visitors with problems of all kinds. As we waited we began to talk about the country, its customs, and the people. He told me his identification had been stolen the night before with all his clothing. He was concerned because he had two guilders plus thirty-five cents in cash and no one to turn to for help except his family in the United States. He didn't want to contact them because he had left home and school in the middle of the last quarter of his second year of college.

We became more than just acquaintances in the next hour. I found he was searching for a meaning to his life and that he felt by getting away from everything he might find it. He thought that the world had far lower ideals than he wanted and he found that most adults he knew were unable to talk about what might be done to correct some of the wrongs that were so apparent.

At last we stood at the counter, and the clerk told him that his check could not be cashed because he had no identification. I offered my credit card but it was refused. As he turned away he said, "I guess I'll have to cable my old man. I really don't want to . . ."

"You're going to need proof of your birthplace and you can't even get back into the United States without another passport. How can I help you?" I asked.

He shook his head, "You can't."

I was able to cash my check, and when I turned to leave he was waiting for me. "Why don't we think a little more about the problem over a sandwich?" I suggested.

"I'll take you up on that. I haven't eaten since yesterday, and then someone gave me an apple," he replied. We sat down at one of the sidewalk tables nearby. I was aware of the people who passed us and turned to look, frown, and shrug their shoulders.

Lack of communication has caused wars and incredible human sufferings, but the dialogue which began between us that day was a form of deep discovery. He told me about his life and how hollow he felt it had been. As a child he had looked up to his father and mother. When they were divorced and he was shifted from one parent to the other he heard nothing but bitterness and began to realize that marriage was "not all that great."

"My dad spent most of his time at the office and the short visits we had together made me realize that he didn't have much of a hold on life.

"My mother used to take me to Sunday school, but I never went after I was seven years old. For years I tried to remember the good feeling I had had when I was in church, but I never said anything to anybody because when I was with the kids we talked of turning everything upside-down and starting things afresh. No one said anything about church, but we did talk a lot about God. Everybody thinks kids don't have any reverence because they see only the revolutionary acts on campus and in the city, but . . ."

We lingered long after the food was gone. When we finally got up I gave him my address and asked him to please let me help. Again he shook his head. "I would like to talk to you again, though. Could we meet tomorrow close to the park? I'll probably stay near there tonight. There are a lot of kids who sleep there every night."

The next afternoon I found him on a bench with his shawl around his shoulders and his bare feet making circles in the grass. We started where we had left off the day before with no embarrassment, no explanations, no excuses.

"Do you believe there really is a God?" he asked. He looked intently at me and the moment seemed like a year. The common "of course I believe in God" answer would not be satisfactory. Much more was needed.

"Many people never come to know God because they expect to find him by going to church and by performing certain religious rites," I began. "I know God myself because long ago I realized that hearing about him from others, reading about what is written of him wasn't enough. I had to find out for myself and the only way I knew was to find a way of talking with him myself." Then I shared the experience I had when I first went off by myself at the age of ten. "God," I had said, "if you really care anything about me and want me to live in your world and try to help people, then you've got to let me know you are there somewhere and that you are real." Then I sat alone in my downstairs playroom with my eyes closed just waiting for something to happen. A warmth ran through my body and I felt suddenly alive as if I had been waiting all of my ten years for this moment.

I knew then there was a quickening Power which answers

to the spirit of the seeker. I didn't see a Being, I didn't hear a voice, but I knew deep inside me that something had happened which I couldn't explain. After that I began to do this often and sometimes I asked advice on schoolwork and my childish problems. I remember clearly talking to God about the jealousy I felt toward a girl. She seemed to have all of the things I wanted—money to spend, red shoes, long curls, and roller skates.

"People don't know God until they are willing to build a personal form of communication. From my childish experiences grew a gradual understanding of God's love and concern. I began to realize that God was not going to set aside the unpleasant things of life because he had given me the right to choose. I knew I could ask for help in making decisions, but I alone was responsible for my acts."

Carl, my barefoot friend, looked at me intently. He got up and I thought, I have failed somewhere. God, let me help.

I took out a couple of sandwiches and we ate in silence. Several other young people in thongs, capes, and dirty jeans joined us. They seemed to know Carl. We talked about war, campus life, and the long line across the street forming for free beer.

All at once they got up. As they started to leave, Carl asked, "How about tomorrow? Same time, same place?"

I nodded and they sauntered off. I went on a bicycle trip that afternoon along one of the polders outside Amsterdam. Everywhere I looked I saw the bravery of the people of Holland who in the face of the encroaching seawater had drained and made new land for themselves and were still doing it. I smelled the freshness of the air, watched children playing. Finally, sinking down on a grassy spot, I came to grips with my myriad thoughts. God *was* real to me, but my acceptance of him had come so gradually it was difficult to sort it out to share with others who had so little.

What had been the turning points in my life? Who were the people who had helped start me in the right directions? Was I especially blessed with parents who were good examples? Had I been born in a less difficult age than Carl? What experiences had kept me wanting to know more about God? Was I different from most young people in wanting association with Deity?

I had to say "no" to most of the questions. I wasn't singled out to be a special person, but I had had a mother whose prime interest was her family . . . who sacrificed to get us to church school and to youth meetings of all kinds. I had also had a dad who was fun and who loved his family. Yes, I had had something Carl had never experienced. Was there any way of making this up to him? Could he go back and start over? Was his world so mixed up that I could never share?

The next day Carl was waiting on the bench again and with him the young people of the day before.

"I told them what we were talking about yesterday," he said. "Now tell us if you can how you know there is a God."

Could I put into words this inner security which had come to be so much a part of my life—a security and trust which had come gradually, and an awakening of the Spirit of God which had so often guided my decisions? The Spirit bore witness to me in such power that I knew I was being used to bring this testimony. I listened to myself as to a stranger, eagerly hearing my own words, never wondering what to say. The words were warm and full of life and hope and love. I heard myself tell about a youth camp when I had heard my first expression of admonition given by the elder in charge of our prayer service. I listened to myself living again the doubts I had about finding a companion to share life happily. I relived testimony after testimony of God's expression in my life.

Someone asked, "Do you believe in life after death?" I

told them about the wonderful experience which came both to my husband and me at the time of his death. When we knew the time was short—minutes away—he had smiled, whispered his love for me, and then looked to the corner of the room, moving his lips and extending his hands. With a look of expectancy and eagerness he just closed his eyes and stopped breathing.

There was silence after that. No one spoke at all. Carl was tossing a pebble back and forth between his hands. "I know what you say is true," he said. "I will never forget this moment as long as I live. I have a feeling inside me that is very funny. Maybe I want to cry . . . I don't know."

We all sat there on the grass knowing that something wonderful had just occurred but not knowing what to do with this newfound experience.

One of the girls said, "I suppose we probably will never see each other again, but I hope that I can find out some things for myself. I have so many questions and so few answers, so far. . . ."

We clasped hands and sat very still, feeling the warmth of human relationships based on something none of us completely understood. Holding hands brought a closeness that excluded all else. The traffic of the street, the people walking by, the noise of a busy city . . . all were lost.

We don't have to go to a foreign country to find mixed-up young people. They are right in our own homes. They are part of our church school class. They live next door. One may even be the girl we sit next to on the bus, the student in the classroom. Let's share our testimony of God and his Son Jesus Christ. This is the light that must be uncovered . . . the light to be set on a candlestick and not hidden under a "bushel."

Spiritual service means giving the best that we have.

CHAPTER TWELVE

"On Kissing Frogs"

Ever feel like a frog? Frogs feel slow, low, ugly, puffy, drooped, pooped. I know. One told me.

The frog feeling comes when you want to be bright, but feel dull. You want to share, but are selfish. You want to be thankful, but feel resentment. You want to be big, but are small. You want to care, but are indifferent.

Yes, at one time or another each of us has found himself on a lily pad floating down the great river of life, frightened and disgusted, but too froggish to budge.

Once upon a time there was a frog. But he wasn't really a frog. He was a prince who looked and felt like a frog. A wicked witch had cast a spell on him. Only the kiss of a beautiful young maiden could save him. But since when do cute chicks kiss frogs? So there he sat—unkissed prince in frog form.

But miracles happen. One day a beautiful maiden grabbed him up and gave him a big smack.

Crash—boom—zap! There he was—a handsome prince. And you know the rest. They lived happily ever after.

So what is the task of the Church? To KISS FROGS, of course. —Wes Seeliger. Reprinted by permission from *Faith at Work,* 1000 Century Plaza, Columbia, Maryland 21044.

It is hard to love the unlovely. Yet if we are to take Jesus as our example this is what we must do. The four Gospels are full of stories about Jesus loving all kinds of people, some of them repulsive, unsavory, self-centered, conniving, loathsome, deformed, or grotesque. Yet his compassion never wavered. He probably never saw their physical or spiritual ugliness, although he knew it was there. He looked beneath the externals and saw the beauty of a child of God. He didn't see frogs; he saw princes.

Are we as Christians really concerned with other people, or are we concerned only with "our kind of people"?

* * *

[14] The first time I signed up as a volunteer for community service I little realized the variety of experiences that would come to my family and me in the years ahead. There was the three-year period when I was "mother" to a hundred or so black, white, and Mexican junior high girls. My own children grew accustomed to the many phone calls and visits that came for "Mrs. T." Crises seem to be daily occurrences for most teen-agers, but for some of these girls the crises were not only real but terrifying. They needed someone with whom they could share their thoughts and feelings. My responsibility was to try to be that someone. I spent hours trying to form a drama club for some of the patients at the Kansas Neurological Center. One teen-age girl who wanted desperately to speak more clearly became my special project. She didn't make much progress with her speech problem, but she also needed a friend, and I was able to fill that need.

There was the home for nonadoptable boys in California which asked for families to volunteer to be friends of these boys—to provide a place for them to visit on weekends, holidays, and special occasions like birthdays. Fifteen-year-old Paul, whose face was covered with acne, was not often invited. He was a strange boy—the kind of strangeness that occurs when there have been too many hurts too early in life. We were asked if we would be willing to take him and we said yes. Paul liked to come and spend long quiet periods at the piano, pecking out tunes, note by note. He seemed to need this time to be alone, and yet not alone.

* * *

[41] Near the turn of the century a young Norwegian boy joined his country's merchant marine corps and shipped out as a crewman. He soon became friends with another young man who served as cook, and they remained close friends for several voyages. Finally Andy left the merchant marines and went to America to earn his fortune. Years later, in New York City, he saw a man stumble out of a doorway and stagger down the street. Although incredibly ragged, dirty, and emaciated, this pitiful drunk resembled his old merchant marine friend. Looking more closely, Andy discovered that indeed it was. Remembering what he had been, Andy took his old shipmate to his room and over many weeks dried him out, nursed him back to physical and mental health, and helped him get a job.

Eventually Andy was financially able to enroll at a seminary and study for the ministry. When a cook was needed for one of the dormitories at Christian College Andy thought of his old friend and recommended him.

The job turned out to be more than just cooking. His kitchen helpers were needy students, and many of them had problems. One young man bitterly resented the poverty that made it necessary for him to work in the kitchen. However, through the love, devotion, and guidance of the cook (the former unlovely drunk) this boy began to see things in a different light. One night he knelt in the kitchen to ask Christ to come into his life. This young man went on to become a minister and later a bishop in his church. His influence for good was widespread.

Many lives were touched directly and indirectly because Andy recognized a drunken bum and wasn't too squeamish or too proud to "kiss a frog."

* * *

Trying to help others isn't always successful. With the best intentions in the world, we often make mistakes. Sometimes our mistakes will be funny; occasionally they will be tragic. Just as love and hate are twin emotions, so do-goodery and meddling may be confused with genuine service.

[42] Lots of people say that helping is fun, but I know for a fact—because I read it in a pamphlet put out by NOW (National Organization for Women)—that not only is helping not fun, but it is actually "a Band-Aid approach to massive social problems."

According to this pamphlet, "Our volunteer time could be spent more profitably in work for political changes to ensure the needed funding for such positions" because "we may be taking the kind of job that would put food on the table for the millions of women on welfare who can't find part-time jobs."

Yet we all realize that legislation and money can't do everything. Sometimes that personal touch answers need as nothing else can. The night my father died a neighbor whom I hardly knew came to our door, and when I opened it, she simply put her arms around me and held me close. I can't imagine any agency helping as she did.

When I was about twelve years old and suffering all kinds

of girlish humiliation because I had to wear a sheepskin-lined brown school coat over everything I owned, a kind lady gave me a tweed coat with a real fur collar. It was not new, but I took it gladly and was happy for what she did.

Yet when my brother and I tried to do the same thing for someone else, it bombed. Some new boys came to our country school wearing bib overalls over their dirty long winter underwear. We had a few things around home that we could no longer wear, so we tied them all together into a neat bundle and lugged them a mile to school, only to have them scornfully rejected by our shirtless but proud young neighbors. "We don't *want* any old clothes," they said.

So there are plenty of problems extant in both giving and receiving. You may think you are kindly, but someone else may think you are a meddler.

Some people, however, are just natural-born "do-gooders" without even trying. I grew up very suddenly, so that at fourteen I was five feet eight inches tall, and very strong and capable looking. From that time on I was constantly being sought out by various neighbors to "stay with mother [a nonwalking diabetic of eighty-eight] until we can hire somebody permanent," "to help Sister Blanding take her weekly tub bath, because she might slip and fall, and you are the only person big enough to hold her up," or "come to our house for three weeks or so to help mind my kids while I wait to go to the hospital for the fourth." In such cases as these I did not actually volunteer. Fate sort of drafted me.

Once after I had my own family there were neighbors who lived near us in North Platte, Nebraska, who seemed to need a tremendous amount of help and counsel. They were charming, literate people, the parents of four children, but nobody could have been more disorganized. The mother, Janet, was a saver. She liked crafts, and every bit of string and every piece of foil looked as if it might be useful someday. Her garage was stuffed from front to back, top to bottom, so tight that if the door was opened things would just stay wedged where they were. The house was a wreck because she and the children were up almost every night—*all* night—fooling around with crafts of one kind or another. The kids seldom got to school on time unless they were prompted by school officials. Hugh, the father, tried to appear neat and useful but the sight of that house and family every night literally drove him to drink. They had been to marriage counselors and ministers. So why did I ever think that I could do anything for them? I spent hours trying to get Janet to plan her daily work and then follow that plan. This all seemed so simple to me, as I am the kind of compulsive housekeeper who will toss away a crumpled Kleenex from the top of the box just to make the box look neater.

I helped with her ironing. I helped her kids learn to read. I listened to the story of her marital problems. I invited the family to picnics in the backyard and tried to encourage the oldest boy to stay in Scouting. Of course when we moved away a few years later the family was much the same. The father was drinking more, the mother was still completely disorganized, and the kids were all failing in school. But I did get one sweet reward from my efforts. It was a birthday cake—seven tiers high—and decorated so magnificently that it rivaled a Buddhist temple. Janet and the kids had spent an entire night baking and decorating it, as they were all learning to decorate cakes that winter.

Once I was committed to spending one day a week cleaning house for a young woman who had been crippled in a car accident. She sat in a wheelchair, and her hands were mostly useless too, but we had good times together. She had loved to cook before her accident but couldn't do it alone afterward, so she would find the recipes and read them off to me while I put the ingredients together. I never cared much for cooking, but in this manner we turned out several gourmet dishes. Other women in our church group also helped her. Each day of the week was assigned to someone. I think we really did do a worthwhile volunteer service for this woman, because without us coming in every day she would have been all alone. Once, before we scheduled our visits, she had fallen out of her chair and had to lie on the kitchen floor until her husband came home from work. But good-naturedly she said, "I had a nap while I was down there."

We kept her company, and probably also saved the family some money. But in doing her work so diligently we unconsciously kept her from developing what few strengths she still had left. Although the same women finally went daily to give her physical therapy, she eventually had to go to a special hospital for care. She just sort of "gave up" on trying.

My husband is a minister, and for several years we used to visit a teen-ager who had been badly burned when he was a child. Time and again he was in various hospitals, and time and again we visited him there, worried about his future, and prayed endless prayers for him. He was in pain most of the time, and he had taken so much medicine his mother thought he was becoming addicted. His health problems were also keeping him from having any kind of normal social life.

Furthermore, all of the members of his family—mother, father, and four brothers—were among the most unlucky people I have ever met. While the mother was having a hysterectomy which they couldn't afford, her husband had back surgery followed by a heart attack; one of the sons was in a car accident; and another was drafted. Then they discovered that termites were eating the foundation from under their house.

We weren't very hopeful for this boy or his family. But several years later he and his wife stopped by our house for a visit (we had moved a long way from them since the hospital days) and he was a changed person. He had a pretty wife, a baby daughter, a good job, and a whole new outlook on life. He came to give us his testimony of how God was taking care of him. Of course the Lord helped him, and he had done a lot for himself, too, but I still felt that our concern and friendship for him over the years had done some good.

So, while helping isn't fun (it is usually a lot of hard work) and while it sometimes doesn't really help, I'm still a do-gooder at heart. There are always lots of personal relationships involved, and the outcome of any situation defies forecast. Some of the worst days of my own life have been those I endured letting people help me . . . but then there is always the memory of that tweed coat with the real fur collar!

Jesus and the disciples went about doing good, but they were either intelligent enough to know what was actually needed or else they waited to be asked. After all, there is a big difference between giving the ministry of angels and making a nuisance of yourself!

Jeri Auerback, who founded Friday Forum, also met some reverses in her experiences of service.

Not all our efforts to help have had good results. An invalid white woman was referred to us as badly in need of help, so Vera and I visited her. Mrs. K. was a widow. She was too ill to work, but not eligible to receive welfare assistance and not old enough to receive social security. She and Marie, an adult mentally retarded daughter, lived on the daughter's welfare allowance of $88 a month plus a food allotment. They needed more than Vera and I could give them, but we did feel we could take Mrs. K. to pick up her food allotment once a month and do other things such as taking meals over occasionally, running errands, or just visiting her. In November each year I took Mrs. K. and her daughter to a department store where we met their social worker and were able to buy new clothes and linens through a city welfare program.

The one thing we really would have liked to help Mrs. K. with was cleaning their little house. Neither had the inclination or the energy to do even the least amount of cleaning. They had long ago pulled things out of closets because of the mice, and clothes were hanging on hooks on the walls and stacked on every available piece of furniture. The kitchen table was crowded with assorted bottles of pills, half-empty jars, papers, odds and ends of every description. It was not only unsightly, it smelled. But whenever we'd suggest cleaning, Mrs. K. had a reason why it couldn't be done.

She was filled with resentment aimed at everyone: the welfare workers were always out to cheat her of what was due her; her daughter wouldn't take her medicine; the doctors weren't concerned about her illnesses and wouldn't renew her prescriptions; neighbors "stole" her chickens out of her yard and tomatoes from her garden. It soon became obvious that we could suggest nothing that would please her, so we stopped offering and just listened.

There were times, however, when I felt that I was able to reach through her bitterness. Once, during the holiday season, I took her and her daughter to a church where Christmas dinner was given to the needy. Both were wearing new dresses and shoes. When we arrived at the church, however, Mrs. K. said she didn't feel well enough to get out of the car, so Marie and I left her and went through the food line, filling their plates with turkey, dressing, gravy, and all the usual holiday food. When we went back to the car with the food, Mrs. K. had tears in her eyes. I wasn't sure whether she was feeling sad or thankful or both. I leaned over and kissed her cheek. She smiled, and I took them back to their cramped, dirty home to eat their holiday meal by themselves.

She's a lonely person; she's sick; she's bitter. She would tell me over and over about her hard life. One time I asked her if we could have prayer together. She said, "You pray." We were both blessed, I feel sure. Often I prayed *for* them, but just that once *with* them.

Eventually, Vera and I had to decide to discontinue our monthly trips. Mrs. K. was being dishonest with us, was taking advantage of our assistance, and—though Vera had not mentioned it to me previously—Mrs. K. was unkind in her attitude toward Vera, a Negro. Regardless of her situation, she knew how to use her telephone to get people to come to her aid. When she found a church group that would give her assistance, Vera and I felt we were not leaving her and her daughter helpless. Just prior to our decision, I had taken them for their yearly buying trip. Among their purchases were half a dozen sheets. I helped check everything with the social worker and the store clerk. I loaded and unloaded the packages at their home. The next day Mrs. K. phoned to say the sheets were not there. I was sure they were, but she worked things out through the store manager to get six more sheets. When I went back to the store to pick them up, the manager said, quite philosophically, "We'll give her the benefit of the doubt."

Mrs. K. is still on my prayer list.

* * *

If God could pick and choose whom to love, many of us would feel uneasy! Instead, he feels for all of us what someone has called "The Anyhow Love: I love you good. I love you bad. I love you anyhow." This is the kind of love we must feel for others . . . even the Mrs. K.'s of this world.

It isn't easy to love the unlovely. It is even harder to go on helping people when they misuse our help or take advantage of us. We may even begin to have second thoughts about the whole concept of service.

Why should I go on helping Glenna? She's not even grateful. I don't mind that so much—although it is nice to feel that people appreciate what is done for them—but she doesn't try to help herself at all. She just takes and takes and takes . . . and then often misuses it. She doesn't try to learn how to care for herself and her house and her family. Why should I keep on trying to help her?

If we have a bad experience in serving our whole attitude can change, yet as Christians we are responsible to God for offering our service freely and gladly wherever it is needed. Likewise, the other person is accountable for the use or misuse he makes of the help he receives.

We have to serve and keep on serving. We can't let opportunists or irresponsible recipients of our service so frustrate and embitter us that we stop reaching out. Perhaps the answer is to find another outlet. If we find that one avenue of service leads to a dead end (as with Mrs. K.) the logical thing may be to let someone else try there while we move over to another street.

The experience of Esther and Luke is a good example. When their daughter was killed in a car accident, they decided to take the money they had set aside for Anne's education and use it to help another young person get through college. They took Betty into their home so that she had free room and board, bought her clothing and books, paid her tuition, and gave her spending money. She became in all but fact their "daughter," with no more than the behavior of a daughter expected of her.

Somehow during the spring semester, Betty became a problem to herself, the school authorities, and her friends. She began staying out late, missing classes, and drinking. Her grades went down, she became surly and uncommunicative. Before the spring semester was over she moved out, and as soon as classes were over, she left college.

Esther and Luke were heartbroken, mostly because Betty was the daughter of old friends and they had long felt a real affection for her. They could have let this episode kill their impulse to be of service to some young person who needed their help. Instead, they chose another way to go. Being a teacher at the local junior high, Esther has ample opportunity to meet youngsters who need help. Every Christmas she takes several of the neediest girls and completely outfits them for the year. One dead-end street simply led her into another avenue of service.

Some people—unhappy creatures—serve others from a sense of duty and thereby miss the whole point of Christian involvement. A Christian serves because he can't help it. Christian love, by its very nature, must move outward. There is no other way for it to go.

How many times do we do things because they are expected of us? How many times do we serve simply because it gives us joy? The famous son of a famous father wrote in his boyhood diary: "Went fishing today with my father. It was the most glorious day of my life." For thirty years on the anniversary of that day he wrote in his diary a glowing comment about that fishing expedition. In contrast his father wrote in his diary: "Went fishing today with my son—a day wasted!" The father never knew that this was the most important single association he and his son would ever share. And he lost his "reward for service" because he missed the joy.

In telling of her experiences, Patricia Lindamood wrote:

"The Lord does not intend for us to serve with a sense of burden. We are to serve with joy and let the burden be his. He can extend to us the additional creativity and insight that will make the difference in meeting needs. No matter what our field of endeavor, if we first study things out in our own minds and then add prayer to our efforts, the burden *can* be his."

"The laborer is worthy of his hire" and the only payment worth earning is not self-satisfaction (that's for duty service) but joy (that's for Christian love). Maureen and Bob Hines understand the difference:

Knowing that our love for each other is real and lasting has contributed to our desire and ability to share our lives with others. We have received far more than we will ever give. Needs I never even realized I had have been filled. Some days when the pace is hectic and we are unorganized confusion, I pray for a short season of quiet to do the things I love to do . . . paint, play the piano, ride a horse, or read. But there is very little satisfaction in any of these things when compared with the joy of having two small hands placed lovingly on my face and hearing a little boy voice say, "Love you, Mommy" . . . or having a little girl whisper, "I'm glad I'm yours."

Any contemplation of Christian service must come full circle. Christian love and Christian service . . . they can't be separated. Awareness must take the form of action or it is not Christian.

Some months ago a newscaster told the tragic story of a car that crashed through a bridge railing and landed right side up in the river below. Somehow the lone woman occupant managed to get out of the driver's seat and stand upright on the top of the car. While she did this, seventy-five people gathered on the riverbank to watch. With only her head out of the water she kept waving her hands and crying, "I can't swim! I can't swim!" While seventy-five people watched, she was swept off the car roof by the current and drowned.

Awareness separated from action is worse than useless—it is callous. It isn't enough simply to be aware of the needs around us. As Christians we must do something to meet those needs. We must be willing to take the risk of personal danger, the risk of failure, the risk of ridicule. With God's direction we must be ready and willing to move out in service to others.

And if God asks us to kiss a frog . . . let's pucker up!

Notes

1. Eric Selden
2. Don Brecken
3. Hazel Moler
4. Charles Massie
5. Mrs. Margie D. Machart
6. *Restoration Outreach* Available from Herald House
7. Paul and Becky Petrie Jim and Dixie Parker
8. Billy L. Landers
9. Velma Katschkowsky
10. Peter Wells
11. Mary and Byrnes Fleuty
12. *Family Safety Magazine*
13 Cecil R. Ettinger
14. Wanda Canaday Talcott
15. Carol Braby
16. Marie Shedd
17. Larry and Elaine Snively Ron Van Fleet, Sr.
18. Maureen and Bob Hines
19. Jan Morris
20. Winnifred Sarre
21. Martha Hamm
22. Rosemary Fishburn

23. Ian Rowett
24. Lela Eskridge
25. Robert G. Fisher
26. Patricia Lindamood
27. Gladys Duffey
28. Phillip R. Legg
29. Donna Wolsey
30. Oka Higdon
31. Wendell Charles
32. Name withheld by request
33. Dale and Sylvia Brush
34. Lillian Millar
35. Santa Fe Stake Office Release
36. Graceland News Release
37. Vida E. Butterworth
38. Carroll and Joy Lindsay
39. From the *Community Observer*, Independence Missouri
40. Ruby Sims
41. Reverend Fedje (father of Dr. Ray Fedje)
42. Alice Bayne